Washington D.C. The Open City

Washington
The
Open
City

D.C.

Photographs by Wolfgang Roth
Text by Guy Friddell
Published by Burda GmbH

"To the Fourth of July, the birthday of liberty in both continents!"

Marquis de Lafayette, September 6, 1825

*Lafayette's response at a dinner
honoring him in the White House after
President John Quincy Adams
had offered toasts to George
Washington's and Lafayette's birthdays.*

Publisher:
DR. FRANZ BURDA

Supervising Editor:
Claus Preute

Layout:
Heinz Roßkopf

Chief of Production:
Heinz Morstadt

Imprimatur:
Kurt Kläger

Layout-Assistance:
Horst Prestenbach
Kurt Lehr
Jan-Bernd Nienborg

Production-Assistance:
Volker Hiß
Dieter Wurth

Pictures on page 92:
The National Gallery of Art;
142: the Department of Defense

© 1974 by BURDA GMBH,
Offenburg
Printed in West Germany

International Standard Book
Number (ISBN): 0-914962-01-9

Distributed by Dietz Press
109 East Cary Street
Richmond, Virginia 23219

Contents

The City in the Sun

Yes, the *open* City.

That word best sums up Washington.

First, the low profile of the city opens it to light and air. All its considerable beauty — and Washington is among the most immediately lovely of American cities — is laid bare.

(Thomas Jefferson, writing in March, 1791 to George Washington, planted the seed of the idea for keeping the buildings low. "In Paris," he wrote, "it is forbidden to build a house beyond a given height, & it is admitted to be a good reservation, it keeps the houses low & convenient, and the streets light and airy...")

Congress reenforced the early regulations by decreeing in 1910 that no structure could be higher than the Capitol. In the absence of thick-set skyscrapers, Washington's eminencies — the Capitol's dome, a crescendo against the blue; the Washington Monument's bold, affirmative stroke, the Jefferson Memorial's high-held arc, the Lincoln Memorial's white block and marching, marble columns — are visible not only from the city's outskirts but keep entering through vistas to its heart.

In views from downtown office windows the Washington Monument, poking over the rooflines of government warrens, seems to look down, mischievously, a playful giant, at the groundlings. A look to the south off a major east-west thoroughfare summons, at the far end of the street, the imposing bulk of the Lincoln Memorial. The Jefferson Memorial's vanilla scoop shifts about among staid rectangles The Capitol dome, as one moves about, fills the sky unexpectedly, crowning backyards and intersections as well as the Hill.

Anywhere in Washington, near or far, a person is apt to be surprised by beauty. Driving east along the George Washington Parkway on the wooded Virginia bluffs, the motorist, at a break in the wall of foliage, glances down the blue-green river and sees, far ahead, spread across the heights on the other side, white on white, many-leveled, the gleaming marble and glistening granite of government.

The city's openness can be appreciated further as being in harmony with an open society. Twenty years ago few blacks were seen, much less employed, in the middle and upper echelons of the District Office, Washington's City Hall. Now the public service, headed by a black Mayor, is fully and amicably integrated.

The District Government itself enjoyed an opening to new powers when, after more than 70 years as a kind of colonial possession at the seat of democracy, it finally gained in 1974 a large measure of home rule. And in the 1970s Congress began operating openly in areas that had been rolled as tight shut as a clinch bug against public scrutiny. Finally, the White House, in the wake of Watergate, seemed determined to be, above all else, open.

The city's cultural resources, well rooted for 40 years, began growing rapidly in the mid-1960s, and, as the Nation's Bicentennial neared, flowered richly, a renaissance. Centered in Washington, the National Endowment for the Arts and a sister organization for the Humanities began stimulating cultural efforts throughout the country.

Finally, Washington always has been open-hearted in offering free access for long hours to its parks, zoo, shrines, monuments, and museums.

During warm months the Washington Monument admits visitors until midnight, and the Lincoln Memorial stays open around the clock all year, flung wide for restless Americans, who, driving through Washington at 2 o'clock in the morning, detour to climb the steps of the Memorial, bathed in light, and look up at the white and shadowed figure of Lincoln, looking down, and then they turn and look at the dark sleeping city and go on.

On "The Hill" the flood-lit Capitol dominates Washington's skyline. Its cornerstone was laid in 1793 and the c

...on dome, weighing nine million pounds, was completed in 1865. The Capitol continues to grow with the country.

At the starter's signal, youths race toward the Lincoln Memorial's broad steps. Completed in 1922, 57 yea

...er Abraham Lincoln's death, the lovely Memorial draws visitors around the clock to the west end of the Mall.

The Monument
to Washington
rises 555 feet

*Framed in cherry blossoms
and surrounded by
sparkling Star-Spangled
Banners, the shaft
honoring George Washington
is the city's tallest
structure, nearly twice
the height of the
Capitol. Begun in 1848,
it was completed
in 1884. Among hundreds
of memorials
in the capital, it is known as
The Monument.*

On a July 4 weekend picnicking beneath the elms on the Mall were Carl and Phylis Wilson of Patuxent River, Maryland, and their guests, Gordon and Sharon Whitmill from DeSoto, Kansas. Their children scampered among the baskets.

Whitmill said they had left home with $400, and, wishing to have something extra going back, "we visit places that are free: the Capitol, the Jefferson Memorial, and the Museum of Natural History and the Washington Monument, which cost only a dime."

On the Fourth, his wife noted, that, too, was free.

"There you go," said Whitmill. "There's another one!"

They had watched the fireworks on the Monument grounds where, said Whitmill, "close to 200,000 people, I bet, were all over the hill and clear down both sides of the reflecting pool to the Lincoln Memorial. You couldn't even see the Memorial's steps. At the close, while the rockets were bursting in the air faster than you could count, the American Flag was outlined down front in red, white, and blue flame. I really did expect to hear the Star-Spangled Banner. I wouldn't have missed it for the world."

What impressed him most?

"The Capitol! Because, you know, no matter what the President or Congress or anybody else does or says, that's the main point of the country. It's what it's all about. That's where the laws come from. Everything has to go through the Capitol. That's the most important part of America."

The city is a perpetual Expo, and the variety and quality of the show made pointless the debate over how and where to celebrate the Nation's Bicentennial. The members of the family simply would come home. While the dispute continued, amid gloomy forecasts that the Nation's birthday party was going to be a farce, the city's great museums went on quietly getting ready, creating exhibitions on the country's origins, preparing for the influx of sightseers.

It is accustomed to being invaded — by Congressmen journeying to and from their districts and in and out of office, blacks in a steady trek from rural America, suburbanites commuting between the inner and outer city, flocks of tourists, numerous as migratory birds during holidays and warm seasons, foreign dignitaries popping up in the President's rose garden, and locust clouds of lobbyists, businessmen, and local and state officials swarming, hat or check book in hand, to the center of power in the United States. Washington is in constant motion, quintessentially America, always on the go.

Yet the visitors' dominant impression of Washington amid all this commotion is one of deep serenity. The swirling tides wash away at the end of the day or the week, and the city in the sun, white and sparkling, is as pure and vulnerable as ever.

That the city is so happily situated is due primarily to three men: George Washington, who picked the site; Thomas Jefferson, who engineered its acceptance by Congress, and Pierre Charles L'Enfant, who designed the city.

The nation's capital, which is dedicated largely to the bargaining of differences, or deals, was born of compromise negotiated between Secretary of State Jefferson and Secretary of Treasury Alexander Hamilton, who usually were opposed as cats and dogs. Two issues were involved.

President Washington favored putting the capital on the Potomac, but Northern Congressmen balked at having it in the South. Meanwhile, the Southern members, most of whose states had paid their Revolutionary War expenses, resisted Hamilton's plan to have the Federal Government assume the states' debts.

Jefferson arranged a dinner with Hamilton and two Virginia Congressmen. Out of it came the agreement that the South would go along with Hamilton's plan for assumption of debts if the North would accept the Potomac site for the capital. It was a nice balancing of interests, although, Jefferson noted later, one of his Virginia colleagues agreed only "with a revulsion of stomach almost convulsive." That was a pity because Jefferson's dinners, thanks in part to his years in Paris, were masterpieces of wines and "savory viands."

In 1790 Congress passed the Residence Bill authorizing the President to select a site "not exceeding 10 miles square on the Potomac" to which the Government would move in 1800. He picked an area within the Y formed by the junction of the Potomac with the Eastern Branch (Anacostia River). It lay 16 miles upstream from Mount Vernon. To do the planning he selected Pierre Charles L'Enfant, an impetuous young French artist and engineer, who had come to America and fought bravely in the Revolution. He was wounded, captured, exchanged, and rose from the rank of Lieutenant to Major. After the war, he designed, among other things, New York's Federal Hall, and the Order of the Purple Heart. A tall young man with an imposing nose and ego, he wrote George Washington that the plan should be drawn on such a scale as to leave room for that "aggrandizement and embellishment which the increase of wealth of the nation will permit it to pursue at any period, however remote."

L'Enfant was gifted, if ever a man was, at seeing the big picture. He produced a master design that would serve a time, "however remote." It was as if, peering through the mists, he foresaw that the wilderness would one day be headquarters for a country of more than 200 million people and at one time or another as many as 20 million a year would wish to visit the capital, see how their country's business was being conducted, and pose on the steps for a picture with their Congressman.

His plan was a mixture of Gallic logic and imagination. Jenkins Hill, a commanding height, "seemed to be a pedestal waiting for a monument." Here he placed the Capitol. He envisioned a Grand Avenue 400 feet wide extending west of the Capitol a mile to a memorial to President Washington. Thus he left room for the Mall. North of the monument on another rise he placed the President's Palace, or house, as the President insisted on calling it. Connecting the President's House and the Capitol was a broad and long avenue, named later for Pennsylvania as consolation for having lost its bid to be the capital.

The Major drew a grid of city blocks and then ran diagonal avenues to connect the main hills directly. The diagonal links, he said, would preserve a "reciprocity of sight." At points where they met on the grid, he planned squares and circles for statues to the young nation's heroes. Today nearly 100 breathing spaces and parks dot the city, and a host of more than 1,000 statues raise swords and palms to passing traffic.

Under L'Enfant's plan, north-south streets are numbered and east-west streets are lettered from the Capitol, and the diagonal avenues are named for the states. The scheme, once understood, permits a person to orient himself quickly.

At any rate, consider what a maze the city would have become without L'Enfant. His plan, laid down in its infancy, stands it in good stead, just as with the individual, psychologists say, the first few years form the character ever after.

Officialdom in L'Enfant's time did not appreciate the magnitude of his contribution. He clashed repeatedly with the three commissioners apppointed to oversee his work. When Daniel Carroll of Duddington, nephew of one of the commissioners, began building a house on a location reserved in the L'Enfant plan, the Major had his force dismantle the offending structure.

The Major, Jefferson reported to Washington, insisted "he had as much right to pull down a house as to cut down a tree." In such conflicts the President sided with the Commissioners and finally, and regretfully, had to dismiss L'Enfant for refusing to accept their authority. The work was carried forward by L'Enfant's assistant, Andrew Ellicott, and a talented free black, Benjamin Banneker.

In 1800, when the Congress moved into the new city, the Major presented a bill for a sizeable sum. Congress rejected it and 10 years later voted him $ 1,394.20. At his death at 71 L'Enfant's belongings were worth only $ 45.

In 1909 his remains were moved from a grave in Prince George's, Maryland to a site on Arling-ton's hillside in front of the Custis-Lee Mansion. Atop the marble tomb was engraved his plan, the main lines of which appear in the noble structures across the Potomac. It was, indeed, a "remote" period, but L'Enfant had become an "embellishment" of the city he shaped and loved.

The capital was a long time taking shape. When President John Adams and the lovely Abigail moved into the White House in 1800, she wrote her daughter that the city was "only so in name." The house was in an unfinished state, with few conveniences; she had to hang wash in the east room. Still, she wrote, it "is a beautiful spot, capable of every improvement . . ."

The city was still capable of every improvement when novelist Charles Dickens visited it in 1842. Sometimes called "the City of Magnificent Distances," it might with greater propriety be termed "the City of Magnificent Intentions," concluded Dickens.

In 1871 Congress instituted in Washington a territorial government with a board of public works, an 11-man Council, and a governor, all appointed by the President, and an elective House of Delegates. To the public works board, President Grant appointed Alexander Robey Shepherd, a 37-year-old free-wheeling contractor quite confident of fulfilling the city's magnificent intentions. He launched a whirlwind program — paving roads and sidewalks, planting trees, lighting streets, burying sewage-laden Tiber Creek, laying out parks — and in three years increased the city's debt to $ 22 million, more than double its legal limit.

Congressional investigations cleared "Boss" Shepherd of personal wrong-doing, but, forced from office, he left Washington for mining ventures in Mexico. He returned in 1897 to a public reception, where he was hailed as the Maker of Washington, "the greatest of her sons." His statue stands in front of the District Building, clutching in the right hand a roll of plans, and looking determinedly on Pennsylvania Avenue, as if the Boss would like to begin all over again.

Of far greater impact on the city than Boss Shepherd's rule was a Congressional reorganization of government in 1878 that placed Washington under three commissioners appointed by the President and responsible to Congressional committees that had final say on the annual budget. Washingtonians were left with no vote and little voice.

Among Congressional leaders who showed concern for Washington's future was Michigan Senator James McMillan, Chairman of the Senate District Committee. In 1901 he sponsored a resolution authorizing a committee of experts to plan improvements in the capital's parks. Serving with him were Daniel H. Burnham and Charles F. McKim, architects; Frederick Law Olmsted Jr.,

Flower-rimmed fountains splash in the President's Park before the South Portico of the White House. Washingto

's oldest public building has been the home of Presidents since John and Abigail Adams moved there in 1800.

landscape architect, and Augustus Saint-Gaudens, sculptor. Their report revived and expanded L'Enfant's plan. It also reflected his vaulting spirit.

Burnham, a designer of the Chicago Exposition of 1893, advised: "Make no little plans. They have no magic to stir men's blood ... Make big plans. Aim high ... remembering that a noble, logical diagram, once recorded, will be a living thing, asserting itself with ever growing insistency. Let your watchword be order and your beacon beauty!"

With that ringing in their ears and Senator McMillan's clout to carry it out, the Committee cleared the Mall of a railroad station and unsightly tracks and laid plans to reclaim 640 acres of swamp for Potomac parklands, landscape Arlington Cemetery and construct Union Station, the Lincoln Memorial, the Federal Triangle of buildings between Pennsylvania and Constitution Avenues, and the Arlington Memorial Bridge.

In ceremonies at Arlington in 1902 marking the reburial of L'Enfant, Secretary of State Elihu Root said, "It is not a change in L'Enfant that brings us here. It is we who have changed, who have just become able to appreciate his work. And our tribute should be to continue his work."

Work continued to make Washington a showplace outwardly, but Congress continued to be oblivious much of the time to the inward needs of the city's population, especially the blacks. That began to change in 1967 when a reorganization provided an appointed Mayor and City Council. In a final breakthrough on December 24, 1973 President Nixon signed a bill, a kind of Christmas gift, granting home rule. On May 7, 1974 the voters approved it overwhelmingly and moved to elect a 13-member Council and Mayor in a September primary and November general election. On January 2, 1975, home rule would, at last, be home.

A combination of factors delayed home rule. Some business interests feared that government costs would rise with selfgovernment. Others thought control of the city would slip away from the white majority. That ceased to be much of an issue when there ceased to be a white majority, and, further, other cities began electing black officials.

Congress had derived some satisfaction from running Washington. Down deep in every Congressman an Alderman is buried. They loved to play with the District budget, the hearings for which were nearly as extensive as those for national defense. But with Congress getting busier and the dynamics of American politics changing, to hold out against home rule became a political liability.

The increase in Washington's black population began with the Civil War. Whenever the United States is in trouble, the capital's population swells, often doubling, as if the nation is putting on

20

SHEPHERD

Boss Shepherd Statue Guards 'City Hall'

Alexander Shepherd became the chief of public works in 1871 and pulled the city out of the mud and ran it into debt by installing sewers and water mains, building sidewalks, paving streets, planting trees, creating parks, and burying the old Tiber Creek. The city went broke – and Boss Shepherd went to Mexico.

21

In Arlington Cemetery the tomb of Major Pierre Charles L'Enfant – engineer, Revolutionary War soldier, visio...

y – looks across the Potomac River to Washington, D.C., the city he designed. On the tomb is engraved his plan.

muscle. In early censuses Washington's population grew at a rate of 7,000 to 17,000 between decades, but reflecting the Civil War, it expanded by more than 56,000 between 1860 and 1870. World War I's demands pushed the increase to more than 105,000. Then under a double draft on the nation's energies, the New Deal program during the Depression boosted the capital's population by more than 176,000 in 1940 and World War II's impact appeared in 1950 through an increase of 139,000 and record population of 802,178 for the District.

The black proportion steadily increased until in 1970 there were 538,000 blacks in the District's total population of 749,000. (Greater Washington's population, including residents of Maryland and Virginia suburbs, contained 702,000 blacks in a total of 2,861,000.) One effect was to promote some white flight from the city leaving Washington with a school system of 130,000 that was 96 per cent black and 60 per cent poor.

To meet that challenge the system began in 1974 to concentrate on every child as an individual, placing the pupil wherever his needs dictated. Thus individuals might be doing reading at one grade level and mathematics at another. The city also planned to open in 1975 a high school for careers in the performing arts and in 1976 one focusing on math and science. When school board members asked the new superintendent, Mrs. Barbara Sizemore, if she could reverse the white flight, she replied that the first obligation was to equip the students already in the system.

"We can't prepare for a population we don't have," she said. "But as we build a system that is responsive to the needs of the student – I don't care who that student is – then in time that structure will be responsive to any student, no matter what his background."

Meanwhile, an increasing number of Washingtonians were not nearly as concerned as some outsiders about statistics. Such bold, uplifting programs as that of public education, plus the prospect of the subway system's completion easing traffic conditions, suggested that the capital would soon enjoy a more pleasant environment than it had ever known. Already municipal services were operating smoothly under a totally integrated force.

"The city works, that's the point," said Ben Gilbert, director of the Office of Planning and Management. Gilbert, who holds the post that L'Enfant could fill, if he were around, is former associate editor and deputy managing editor of the *Washington Post*. "I think people fear what they don't understand," he said. "Let me point out what I like to call the real city of Washington.

"Suppose you erased all political boundaries and let the logical economic growth determine the city. In the early 1800s the real city of Washington was below Florida Avenue in what was then called Boundary Street." He crossed the room and pointed to a map. "By the Civil War the real city had grown almost to where the forts were established. Then by the 1920s it filled the diamond of the original 10 square miles. In the mid-1950s it was filling the area embraced by the Beltway around Washington, and today –" Gilbert paused and spread his arms wide – "it fills this whole wall, extending into the suburbs of Maryland and Virginia.

"If you trace the racial breakdown," he continued, "you will discover that for most of Washington's history, it varies from 20 per cent to 30 per cent black, and the high point is the decade between 1860 and 1870 when it reached 33 per cent. Today it's 29 per cent. I'm speaking of the entire area – greater Washington. So in looking at the city as an economic and social reality, as a place to live, this isn't any different than any major American city and never has been.

"Of course, we have problems of housing, jobs, and education, but with home rule we will be moving even faster toward solutions. This is going to be a very attractive place in which to live, so attractive that an important element in the black community feels that the whites are going to crowd out blacks, as happened in Georgetown. That changed because the market place determines who can afford what kind of house. There's a danger in parts of town of affluent people buying out those who can't afford to pay the rising taxes. I don't think it's going to occur, but city government has the job of creating housing so people won't be just pushed into new slums," Gilbert said.

Meanwhile, there are impressive indications in Washington of blacks steadily advancing, one generation over another, in education and employment.

"That's one of the exciting things about this town," said Gilbert, "and it's a part that is hard for the average tourist to sense. The old idea of the melting pot – we never really had a melting pot in the United States. What we had was an arrangement whereby people of diverse backgrounds could come together, live together, and develop the country. And to a great extent that's happening in this city. There's a strong overlay of one ethnic group – but that isn't unusual either. You can go through this country and find that one ethnic group or another has put its stamp on a particular city. The Irish developed Boston, but today probably more Italians are there than Irish. It's in the American concept. It's a part of this city and it's something that's outside the experience of many who come here from other parts of the country; but I don't know but what it's the most important thing we have to show."

Parades, Picnics, Pigskins, and Pandas

Pennsylvania Avenue is called, with justification, "the most historic avenue in America."

But except for what lies at the opposite ends of its central section – the Capitol and the White House – Pennsylvania Avenue is not so much noted for what is on it as it is for what goes along it.

The Presidents, after being sworn into office at the Capitol, travel the mile and a half to take up their responsibilities in the White House.

Pennsylvania Avenue is made for parades.

Its north side is a hodgepodge of shops and good-sized buildings, but on the south, row on row, are the gray, shouldering, cliff-like, government buildings in the Federal Triangle, a perfect backdrop for marching columns. Those buildings are at their best during parades.

At the White House end of the Avenue is the Treasury Building's imposing bulk, a magnificent photographers stand from which a camera can take in the entire length of the parade with the Capitol, a hill upon The Hill, spreading white and wide in the background.

The Treasury Building is a blot on L'Enfant's plan, partly blocking the vista between the executive and legislative seats. There was a dispute over where to place it, and, the story goes, President Andrew Jackson, walked out, stuck his cane in the ground, and said to put it right there.

And there it is. A parade, at that point, has to take a smart turn to the right, and it is a pleasant sight to see the streaming column of soldiers, bands, floats, flowing massively between banks of humanity on each side of Pennsylvania Avenue, crook in front of the Treasury Building and start uphill.

At the foot of the Treasury Building on Pennsylvania Avenue is lovely Pershing Square, or rhomboid, filled in season with tulips big as teacups, white, ruby red and yellow, a green oasis abloom with flowers and graced by benches in the busiest part of town. But bureaucracies are nervous about unfilled spaces, and the Interior Department would like to plank a building there, the better to define Pennsylvania Avenue, it asserts. It would define it all right, adding one more monolithic wall, closing another invitation to communication among people and pigeons. Interior ought to be resisted.

At the top of the hill the parade turns left on Pennsylvania Avenue and passes the White House. The first thing that the United States requires of a new President after he has promised to save civilization is that he watch, standing for the most part, a parade running two to four hours.

Perhaps the nation considers it inspiring to the Chief Executive. In a way it is like watching the country reel by. There are the gaudy state floats: Louisiana with a giant horn in gold foil celebrating the Birth of the Blues; Massachusetts presenting sober clad Pilgrims, and Colorado offering a ski slope, featuring, one time, a skier who took off in the center of the run, overshot the trailer, and landed with a clatter, unhurt, in Pennsylvania Avenue. But he did that only in front of the President's stand.

The small-town bands, mainly from high schools and colleges give the Inaugural Parade its zip. How many pancake dinners does a town consume to finance the trip? The units come out of the dusk and cold, blowing for all they are worth, the drum major and majorettes high-stepping, bloom a moment in the orange artificial sun of the kleig lights and the President's smile and then are gone – bright, soon-faded quadrennials.

Riding along Pennsylvania Avenue from his Inaugural, John F. Kennedy noted the shabbiness of the Avenue's north side and determined, even then, to change it. He initiated a Cabinet-level study, which concluded that instead of being the city's great thoroughfare, Pennsylvania Avenue "remains a vast, unformed, cluttered expanse at the

Traffic fills Pennsylvania Avenue under the aegis of Freedom, the bronze statue atop the Capitol's dome. Ever

26

President since Jefferson has traveled, after the Inauguration, the mile between the Capitol and the White House.

heart of the nation's capital." The President appointed a Pennsylvania Avenue Commission, headed by Nathaniel Alexander Owings, to rejuvenate the Avenue.

One depressing influence on the Avenue is the Federal Triangle of massive office buildings, proposed at the turn of the century by the McMillan Commission. Alone each is not unbearable. Some are even handsome. In the least prepossessing is some redeeming feature of interest. The headquarters for the Internal Revenue Service, for instance, is banded by huge incised blocks, like spaces to be filled on one's income tax. Form unconsciously follows function. But clumped together, critics say, the wedge of buildings forms a psychological barrier between the Mall and Pennsylvania Avenue.

Tourists are not tempted to leave the green grass and scale the gray heights to Pennsylvania Avenue. And many Washingtonians, sadly, view tourists as strange tribes and would just as soon they remain on the other side of the plateau. They thereby cut themselves off from amenities all along the Mall.

By brightening the north side, the Commission hopes to create a bridge for exchange between the two Washingtons. A beautiful feature at the Avenue's south end, the reflecting pool in front of the Capitol, already has been completed. The new east building of the National Gallery of Art, a handsome glass-sided, fountain-graced pair of triangles, is a work of art itself, enlivening the Avenue and occupying a prominent place at the foot of the Capitol.

A tree-shaded market square and arcades, among other features, would pull tourists and Washingtonians into fraternizing. Curiously, one feature of the plan, proposed removal of the vacant Willard Hotel, has met universal opposition by civic, cultural, and business interests.

Dating from 1901, the present Willard is on the site of an earlier one in which, Julia Ward Howe, seeing the Union troops' campfires during the Civil War, was inspired to write the "Battle Hymn of the Republic." Today's defenders show the same grim determination to save the Willard. The handsome, thick-walled structure, a mellow pear color in the sun, still has the makings of the fine hotel that it once was – and should be again in view of predictions of 35 million tourists annually by 1980.

In his quest to rehabilitate Pennsylvania Avenue President Kennedy was accompanied by Labor Secretary Arthur Goldberg. Inspecting his scattered domain, Secretary Goldberg discovered that the farther he got from headquarters the grubbier the buildings became. Perhaps, he suggested to the President, the Labor Department should bring all its divisions into a new building. That opened on Pennsylvania Avenue in 1974.

Washingtonians fish below the Chain Bridge in the Potomac

In early April herring and shad swim up the Potomac River to find quiet pools in which to spawn. Perch follow the smaller fish, and people follow the perch, and the fishing is good all along the river. A favorite spot for hundreds is the rocky stretch near the Chain Bridge. With luck, a fisherman can net 10 dozen herring in half an hour, plus shad.

The evening sun touches the towers of Georgetown University, a citadel of learning on the Potomac River

luffs. Founded in 1789, directed by the Jesuits, the school is the oldest Catholic university in the United States.

*The Washington Redskins'
veterans exercise,
below, during summer work-
out at Georgetown
University. The Redskins
came to Washington
from Boston in 1937 and
won the fans' hearts.
At bottom, youths play
softball on a field
in one of the dozens of parks
and playgrounds in
the District of Columbia.*

Amateurs and pros enliven the city's fields with sports of all varieties

*The redheaded quarterback
of the Washington
Redskins, 40-year-old
Sonny Jurgensen,
looks downfield, preparing
to pass the football
during summer drills. In*
*1972, the Redskins,
led by Coach George Allen,
played in the Super
Bowl and lost to Miami
– but they will
return, their fans believe.
'The future,' Coach*

Allen has said, 'is now.'
The present is
strenuous enough for gov-
ernment clerks
playing rugby on a city
field. The Washing-
ton Monument is the goal.

The avenue of history obviously is on its way to even greater glory. Meanwhile, there always are the parades.

In the midst of the city is another avenue, a broad green one, Rock Creek Park, traveled by squirrels, raccoons, foxes, and rabbits as well as people.

"To Rock Creek there is nothing comparable in any capital city of Europe," Lord Bryce said.

Extending four miles from Maryland to the National Zoological Park, it comprises more than 1,800 acres lining the winding, rock-filled creek.

On a recent day, among 70 spots for picnicking, one grove especially was animated with families, a dozen or more, it seemed, as many as 50 persons filling the scene with laughter and talk. The fragrance of charcoal filled the air.

On the fringe a trestle table was presided over by an elderly dignified black man, trimly built, shoulders set back squarely, gray hair clipped close, neat and cool in a sport shirt.

Was this his family at the table?

He waved his hand around the grove. "Everybody here's in the family," he said.

All these people kin? Was this a reunion?

"Yes, all one family – our three sons and four daughters and their husbands and wives, children, grandchildren, and great-grandchildren."

He was John D. Bailey, 79. In 1917, at 18, he left Opelika, Alabama, "my birth home," and went with his wife, Amanda, to Everett, Mass. to work a year in an ammunition factory and then came to Washington to work with government agencies.

In Opelika he had finished the eighth grade, which was "high for the time," and raised cotton, corn, and black-eyed peas.

Of their seven children, one, Delois Simpson was a housewife. The others – Louise, Charles, and William Bailey, and Josephine Douglas, Elsie Hunt, and Christine Davis – either worked for or were retired from government departments.

Bailey called to a tall, handsome youth, his oldest grandson, Joseph Douglas Jr. He has a master's degree in public administration from Harvard, Bailey noted, and is Deputy Director of Washington's Department of Human Resources.

From earnings of more than 50 years Bailey has two houses,

"Debt free," said Mrs. Bailey.

What did he feel about Washington?

"I love it well," he said. Looking around at the activity in the grove, he added, unexpectedly, "If it weren't for my children, I'd go back to Alabama to make the rest of my life."

Had he relatives there?

"Two distant cousins."

Why would he go back?

"I was raised up there from a boy," said Bailey, "and I know how to handle Alabama."

How Green Is Rock Creek Park winding through the D.C.'s heart to Maryland?

A mile-wide wooded valley, stretching from Georgetown into Maryland's suburbs, Rock Creek Park was set aside by Congress in 1890 as "a pleasuring ground for the benefit and enjoyment of the people of the United States." They enjoy the 1,800 acres by hiking along 15 miles of trails and riding horses over 14 miles of bridle paths, playing tennis and golf,

picnicking in 70 groves, going to the zoo, or watching animals and birds in their native habitat, or simply, as above, resting at ease amid the greenery. Only careful land-use in Rock Creek's basin, especially Montgomery County, can save the Park "for the people."

Washington Mayor Washington at work

Walter E. Washington, Washington, D.C.'s first Mayor in modern times and its first black chief executive, is able to get along with anybody, said a former U.S. Senator from Virginia, who served on the governing District Committee.

"And moreover," added William B. Spong Jr., "he can persuade just about anybody to get along with everybody else; and that's fortunate because when he took office he had to bring together a city fragmented along racial and economic lines."

Does he, indeed, get along with everybody?

Washington, at his desk in the Mayor's office, pondered.

"I would hope so," he said. "I try to, very hard. That's a part of the equipment. In a city your basic responsibility is first to try to understand a variety of situations affecting people in a community and then try to bring them all into mechanisms of cooperation and unity. It's the theme that I've tried to build. Togetherness is the key word. To the extent to which you can develop that in any community, you have a foundation for building stability and progress – which is really what a community is about.

"I think we have succeeded to a very great degree. In the city we have harnessed individuals and interests that never believed they would be working together."

Born in Dawson, Ga., Washington spent his childhood in Jamestown, N.Y. His mother died when he was 7. His father, a laborer, was determined the son would get a good education. At Howard University, where he received his B.A. degree and headed the student council and varsity athletic club, Washington met and married Bennetta Bullock, a student majoring in education. Then, while working for the National Capital Housing Authority, he attended night classes at Howard and received a law degree in 1948. In 1961 he became Executive Director of the Capital Housing Authority and

in 1966 Chairman of the New York City Housing Authority. In 1967 he heard that President Johnson was considering him for the newly created job of Mayor-Commissioner of the District.

One night at 10 o'clock the President telephoned him in New York and invited him to the White House for a talk.

He had some matters before him, replied Washington, but he would, of course, come to the White House. What day would the President like to see him?

"Take the 7 o'clock shuttle," said Johnson, "and if you have any trouble with that, let me know."

The next day, said Washington, he stayed with Johnson four hours "as the President talked about his dreams for the city. Off and on, when he turned to other business, I would wait in the Cabinet Room. Once, while he was conferring with New York Mayor John Lindsay, I was shifted from the Cabinet Room to the Fish Room, and, when that became needed, to the Press Secretary's Office; and, meanwhile, President Johnson and John decided they wanted me in their conference and came looking in the Cabinet Room. That started a search and a good deal of laughter."

Johnson advised Washington at length on how to get along with Congress and then, in parting, exhorted his nominee: "Work just like you're elected!"

Washington went to work in 1967. Four months later riots erupted in the District's streets after the assassination of Martin Luther King Jr. on April 4. The Mayor directed the military and police to refrain from using guns unless attacked; and when the military proposed to put a curfew on some sections, the Mayor, reasoning that the entire District was affected, insisted that the ban be city-wide for even-handed law enforcement. With these and other judgments he guided the city back to normal in three days.

In the next three years his

administration spent $1 billion modernizing the city's physical plant, eliminating such antequated public schools as "Shameful Shaw" and "Hideous Hine," building libraries, clinics, and playgrounds in neglected areas, and extending municipal services equally to all communities.

"His insights into a complicated city are remarkable," said an aide. "Knowledgeable officials will bring in plans that appear in perfect order, cleared by every department, and the Mayor will take one look and ask if a certain agency or person has been consulted; and so you check and find an element has been missed."

Early in President Richard Nixon's administration Federal officials, preparing to cope with a sizeable antiwar demonstration, planned to confine it to Lafayette Park directly across from the White House. They would, they decided, line up buses as a barrier.

Washington listened to their views and then asked: "Anybody who goes over those buses and tries to break into Pennsylvania Avenue, you're going to tear-gas, is that right?"

That, the others agreed, was the strategy. At that point, an aide says, Washington said, "All right, what are you going to do if they start for the White House or turn uptown?"

The law enforcement officials decided to let the demonstrators use the ample grounds around the Washington Monument, which they did, peacefully.

Of Washington's apparently unconquerable good nature, a District official noted that the Mayor's programs had to win support from the White House, the Capitol, the business community, and the citizenry. He couldn't hold together all those factions by pounding tables.

One night the Mayor will speak to 2,500 blacks in a Baptist Church and the next he will be one of a half-dozen blacks at a Georgetown party, the Washington-watcher observed. "He

"To talk about a city becoming a model for a nation is good, but to implement the idea is something else," says Walter Washington, Mayor of Washington.

At a picnic in Rock Creek Park, Robert and Amanda Bailey, who left an Alabama farm 57 years ago for Wa

on, sit for a family portrait. Bailey and six of his seven children found careers with government agencies.

moves constantly from one segment of town to another, and that's part of the business of pulling the city together, making sure that even with the segments that don't know each other, a common link is the personality of Walter Washington.

"At one of those formal Georgetown parties a woman came up to him, handed him a plate, and said she'd like some of this and that dish, and he obligingly filled the plate and handed it to her. Half an hour later she was apologizing that she hadn't realized he was the Mayor. He didn't want to embarrass her, but she learned something in the process. He's not a man who wears his race on his sleeve, but he's proud that he's black."

Even more important than masonry, Washington believes, is the building of understanding among people. "You create ways through which they can live and work together and this becomes the foundation of a city," said the Mayor.

Is much more expected of the capital than other cities?

"Visitors from all around the country come here and admire the great monuments and look on this city as the ultimate, as though one piece of turf in America is a place where perfection must abound. But living behind the monuments are human beings of all persuasions, with hopes and needs for housing, education, and jobs that people everywhere experience.

"To talk about a city becoming a model for a nation is good, but to implement the idea is something else. The key to it is to get all the diverse parts working together toward a common goal of a better city. I'm optimistic about my city, and I never give up hope on anybody. Every person has a worth, and we try to move in that positive vein, trying through some program to give each his place in the sun. We don't always make it, but if we keep driving at it, we get closer."

Katherine Graham publishes "The Post"

After *The Washington Post* printed the Pentagon papers and opened Watergate, some magazines called the newspaper's publisher, Mrs. Philip Graham, "Katherine the Great." But the *Post's* people refer to her as "Kay Graham," in whom there's nothing of the potentate. Chairman of the board of the company that includes the *Post, Newsweek,* and a broadcasting division, she manages those multiple responsibilities and remains a warm, direct individual.

"In that sort of role," said an associate, "some women can only cope with the fact that they are boss by adopting kind of mannish, aggressive ways. And she has not got any of that, as you will observe."

Tall, brown-eyed, she has a flair for style in dress. Her face, absorbed in a serious discussion, will suddenly be lighted by a smile that borders on being, if not reckless, daring.

From the time she became publisher after her husband's death in 1963, she has been "steadily learning and gaining confidence and making tough-minded decisions," said a fellow newspaper executive, "and today the Post is much stronger than ever."

What prepared her for the job as publisher?

"I wish I had been better prepared," she said. "What little preparation I had came from living with people – my husband and my father – who were deeply involved with running it and both of whom were rather communicative about their problems and what they were doing."

She had worked on campus publications at Madeira School and Vassar and then a year as a reporter in San Francisco and later, at her husband's urging, four years writing for the *Post's* Sunday Department, and editorial page and a year on the circulation department's complaint desk.

"But those jobs weren't involved in management, and the difference between hearing about management and doing it is the same difference as watching somebody swim and swimming," she said.

Assuming the role of publisher was "like putting one foot in front of another. I realized that all these men were running departments and wanted me – told me in fact that I had to take charge. But I viewed it as a sort of holding operation, that I'd be a kind of family hand and they'd go on running it – which, of course, never works. I suppose I really didn't know the right questions to ask, or maybe I wouldn't have done it. But we were a smaller company then, and so, with a lot of help from other people, it worked."

Her parents were strong, "driving, striving" figures. Her father, Eugene Meyer, was concerned with his five children's activities and deeply interested in how they were doing at school. "He was very demanding," she said. "He liked us to get good marks." Her mother, Agnes, communicated her wide range of interests and rigorous standards to them. "She insisted that we work. She didn't care what we did when we grew up, but we had to do something. The idea that you could, say, just get married and sit back, didn't occur to you."

In turn, the Grahams set similar values for their own four children, one of whom, Don, joined the company in 1971. Earlier, in a style reminiscent of his parents', he set about learning about Washington by working two years as a member of the city police department.

"My husband, obviously, was the most formative influence of any," said Mrs. Graham. "I certainly learned more from him about a range of things. He was an extraordinary figure and a magic one. He just swept people along with him. He was articulate, brilliant, and very funny; and had enormously creative and advanced ideas. For instance, he

and President Johnson were close for several years, and later, going through his papers, the President found a letter from Phil, written to him when he was Vice President, outlining ideas for the Great Society.

"So he raised my sights. He helped me work. In fact, he wanted me to work more than I did. I learned how to enjoy life with Phil. Before, I was hung up on the complexities and difficulties and saw the negative a great deal. And I guess I really learned how to laugh with him. Which I think I value more than anything.

"Trying to create first-rate editorial products is tremendously rewarding in the sense that this is what you're about. Under the First Amendment a newspaper has the responsibilitiy as well as the opportunity to do the best kind of reporting possible to inform people.

"What interests me as much is the business side. In speaking to business analysts, I make the point that good first-rate editorial products, while they may create problems if you're doing your job, are in no way contradictory to a well-managed profitable business. In fact, one depends on the other. If you don't run the business well, you can't maintain those editorial organizations. You've got to be strong and profitable, or you can't do the kind of reporting we did on Watergate. To turn two reporters loose on one story for 10 months, as we did with Watergate, is expensive just to begin with, and to take the flack that investigative reporting creates requires a lot of economic strength."

"Under the First Amendment a newspaper has the responsibility as well as the opportunity to do the best kind of reporting possible to inform people," says Mrs. Graham.

41

What did she view as the nation's number one problem?

"The most obvious one is a shaken confidence in government. But probably more serious than that are the economic problems. But the noticeable thing is that the system is working even under incredibly difficult circumstances. We're resilient and there are an incredible number of exciting, wonderful people in this country. When called upon, they rise to an emergency. As for our leadership, I feel we are in a transition. We have worn out a very old group of leaders, so the younger Governors and political leaders have to rise to the top."

Had any public figures impressed her particularly?

"John F. Kennedy was very exciting, but he had still to prove whether he would have been a great President. Bobby, his brother, had great passions about decency. Of course, again, he didn't have time to develop. In retrospect, I believe President Johnson would have been a very great President, but for Vietnam. The Texas frontier is an interesting and complex part of the country, and he was a mirror image of it. But that wretched war ruined him. Now he's coming into perspective again."

She paused, and then, with a laugh, said, "You know, he didn't speak to me for five years. Not even in a receiving line for 2,000, he wouldn't say hello. It's so funny, but it's so typical."

Why was he upset?

"Whoever is President always gets upset at the press in general and the *Post* and *Newsweek,* in particular because we're publishing right under his nose. He was just very angry. And then about a year after he had gone to the ranch he came back suddenly and we had a wonderful reunion – after which the *Post* wrote something else that upset him, and he went back to not speaking. And I was sad. But that's the price you pay for this job. It doesn't make you that many friends – nor should it."

George Allen looks to Super Bowl

Set amid Virginia's green pastures near Dulles Airport is the Washington Redskins' headquarters, which couples the efficiency of an assembly line with the dedication of a monastic order.

And set on a chair in the conference room was a helmet of gleaming burgundy, bare as Yorick's skull.

But nothing of Hamlet's indecision was in the room.

Instead, atop a television set was a sign: IS WHAT I AM DOING OR ABOUT TO DO, GETTING ME CLOSER TO MY OBJECTIVE ... WINNING?

The expounder of that school of thought, Head Coach and General Manager George Allen, entered from his adjoining office. Tall, trim, still dark-haired at 52, he strides, shoulders hunched slightly forward, like a halfback ready to take the ball on an end sweep.

In two years, after coming from the Los Angeles Rams in 1971, he hustled the Redskins to a league championship and to the Super Bowl.

How long had he been involved with football?

"Nearly all my life, starting way, way back when I was just a kid in Detroit. I felt if you could make a living coaching, that's like being paid for playing a game."

What is a football player's single most important trait?

"Attitude is first in my mind. Course, he's got to have ability, but if he has ability and doesn't have attitude, he's not going to do it."

What does a head coach need?

"Lots of patience. And you certainly can't be lazy. Because there's not enough hours in the day to do all the things you have to do. You got to be a hard worker, and you got to know what to do. You know, you can work hard moving a pile of dirt from here to here."

And what's a coach's most important trait?

"A deep desire to win. And nowadays you have to motivate other people, and much more than in the past."

The quiet-spoken answers came swiftly, like signals at the line.

How do you motivate people?

"I don't know. You just get to know the other guy as much as you can and see what makes him tick. It depends on the individual and his background."

The face is boyish and shrewd, the voice husky and clipped.

Do Washington fans differ from others?

"They've been unusually appreciative, maybe because they've been down so long. They appreciate what's taken place the last three years.

"And this is a good football area. They like the contact sport. The type of people we have here want aggressiveness, whether it's Republicans or Democrats or blacks or whites, or whatever it is. They like the aggressive arena-type of sports."

Did he think that Washington's being a politicians' town, dependent on campaigns, inclines it to football?

"I think winning football. Winning football, right.

"I also think one thing the Redskins have done is bring this area together. This is something they all have in common: Pull for the Redskins."

Why did he select the area?

"I picked this because of my friendship with Jack Kent Cook and my respect for Ed Williams, and I saw it was a franchise that could be rebuilt into a winner and Washington would be an exciting place to live in. So that's why we picked it."

To what did he attribute his drive to win?

"Oh, I don't know. I wasn't a real good athlete. I could do a lot of things well and played all sports, but I never did anything exceptionally well. I think that somewhere in me there's a drive to get others to realize their potential by hard work and being

"Somewhere in me there's a drive to get others to realize their potential by hard work and being organized," says Coach George Allen of the Redskins.

organized. I think it's just that I realized you can do almost anything you want if you work hard enough.

"We were very, very poor, and I never even thought I could afford to go to college."

They all worked – his father in Detroit's plants, his mother taking care of children, and young George as a messenger for Chrysler Corporation, a gardener, a worker in a trailer factory.

"My mother has a lot of determination and drive, and I may have gotten that from her. My dad was sick part of the time and she kept the family together and did some things that showed me she had leadership."

When he was coaching at Morningside College in Sioux City, Iowa, he met and married Etty Lumbroso, who was acting in a community theater. They have four children.

"She's a wonderful wife and mother," he said. "To be the wife of the kind of coach I am you really got to have patience because I come home at different hours and she can't plan much of a schedule, and she's bringing up the children more than I am. She designed and practically built the home we just moved in."

How did he relax from the tensions of coaching?

"By working out."

What are his long-range aims for the Redskins?

"Win the Super Bowl!"

"That's not only long-range, that's in the immediate range," he added. "Get a larger stadium. Build our own dynasty. We already have one started."

He had sandwiched the interview between contract talks and a trip to New York. Now he rose and shoved the cushioned swivel chair under the conference table.

"Let's put these chairs back," he said. "What I always do is make everyone put the chairs back. Otherwise it looks messy."

In his drive to win, George Allen wasn't leaving any detail, even the chairs, out of place.

John Gardner seeks open government

Sitting in his back yard in Washington, with a mockingbird going on at a great rate in the background, John Gardner, founder and head of Common Cause, said for years he had wondered why somebody didn't start a citizens organization.

"Every time I read about special interests putting across some bill that wasn't in the public interest, I wondered why somebody wasn't there saying, 'What's good for the country? What's good for the taxpayer?' But then I became Secretary of Health, Education and Welfare, and I began to see that citizens action could be pretty effective. It was the citizens groups that worked me over. They made me listen. I began to do a little reading and found that back to the time of the Colonies this had been an ingredient in American life. Look at populism or the suffragette movement or the abolitionists, and you see that it comes out of different segments of the populace, not the people collectively with a capital P but from different segments. The lakes are dying and the rivers are drying, but if we had waited for the political parties to tell us, we'd still be waiting. The story came from people who were so determined they were hard to sit next to at dinner. They really went after you. And I looked at this and said there's something here to work with. I learned a lot as Secretary of HEW."

President Johnson appointed him to HEW in 1965 and informed him of his intention just before Gardner, then chairman of the White House Conference on Education, introduced him to a session of 1,000 delegates.

"We had talked twice, and I could tell something was on his mind, and that day the band was playing, and as the President came up on the platform, he took my hand and kind of turned me away from the audience, and said, 'If I offered you a real big job, you wouldn't turn it down, would you?' His first mention of it was right there in front of a thousand people, whispering to me.

"He was an extraordinary person, a man who wanted to do things right. He really did. He had a very deep feeling about the job and history. He wanted to do the best he could, I never doubted that. As the years pass I look back with increasing feeling about his commitment. He was the first President ever to say that education was the number one priority, and that had a big impact. In this government, if the President gives the green light, it's go. The President is a tremendous energizer. A lot of things happened because he was there saying, 'I'm with you. Keep moving.' He let us think up the ideas, and he was there with the support. He got caught in one of history's traps. Whoever had been President would have been trapped, in my opinion, by that war."

Might not another President have stopped it?

"Years back the series of moves might have been stopped, but I suspect that any President would have made about the same initial moves Johnson made. The whole history from Hitler moving into Czechoslovakia to 1960–'63, was in the mould of mutual security – the cold war, the conception of how one dealt with aggression that finally proved to be something other than we thought it was. But he was not the only one slow to learn that lesson. Practically his whole generation was slow to learn it."

To start Common Cause, Gardner simply announced that he was beginning a citizens movement, "the riskiest thing I ever did because if no citizens had showed up, it would have been a very public stumble. The letters just began to pour in, 200 the first day and, by the end of the week, a thousand a day, and we had to rush and get ourselves a name and a dues structure, and it just took off. We set $100,00 as a goal for the first year; we got it in 23 weeks.

"We had 175,000 members the first year and rose as high as 230,000. Then we began to lose momentum and dropped during the '72 primaries and bottomed out in August at 196,000 and then began to climb slowly until Sam Ervin went on the tube, and then the membership just soared to the ceiling. Our first drives for openness in government were before Watergate. We had occupied the territory not knowing that would break.

"We are concentrating on what we call the process-of-structure issues — making government more accountable, responsive, and accessible to citizens. And it's a great formula because once you open up government, it's as much a service to conservatives as it is to the liberals, the blacks, the whites, the rich and the poor. Insist a city council open up, and it serves all kinds of citizens.

"If we open up Congress and break up the rigidified leadership of the chairmen, we're going to have a considerable period of vitality. Of course, somebody always has too much power, and although we're moving power away from the chairmen and toward the leadership and the caucus, sure as we're sitting here somebody 10 years from now is going to be trying to get the power away from the leadership and caucus because they have too much. It's a constant losing and regaining of balance.

"My members think, you know, that we'll get Congress in perfect shape and then go home and forget about it. It will never happen. Power is dynamic, always shifting. Watching it, you lose it. Give it to one person and he begins to abuse it. That's life."

"We are concentrating on making government more accountable, responsive and accessible to citizens," says John Gardner, who directs Common Cause.

45

Gardner was born in Beverly Hills, "a dinky little town then, a good place in which to grow up." His father, an Englishman and real estate broker, died at 29, and his mother reared the "close family" of four boys – two brothers and two cousins. She was "a very strong and able woman and put us through college buying, renovating, and selling houses."

Gardner earned his B.A. and M.A. degrees at Stanford University and his Ph.D. at the University of California. He dropped out of Stanford two years "to write the Great American Novel" and in his senior year married a girl of "extraordinary grace and beauty," Aida Marroquin from Guatemala. They have two daughters.

When they met, she spoke no English, and Gardner could not converse in Spanish.

"But it was a negligible barrier," he said.

He taught psychology at the University of California, Connecticut College for Women, and Mount Holyoke College. In 1943 he joined the Marines and served with the OSS in Washington, Italy, and Austria. He joined the Carnegie Corporation in 1946, became president in 1955, and did a series of consulting jobs for the government until Johnson appointed him to HEW.

Did he have any hobbies?

"Common Cause is my hobby. It's just enormously interesting. It's my avocation, my vocation. I have been lucky enough most of my life, certainly for the last 25 years, that my work has been my hobby."

As he discusses the citizens movement he makes shaping gestures with his hands, balls his fist, flings his arms wide.

"If we establish once and for all the idea that people have a right to know how their taxes are decided and how committees and other things work, if people really got it through their heads that openness is a deterrent, this would be revolutionary" he said.

"Accountability is a pretty easily understood thing; but you can't hold your government to account if you don't know what they're doing; yet, very few Americans would have said a year ago that openness in government is important. We are inserting that into the political thinking of the country, and once we get it there, it's going to be awfully hard to get out. The same goes for accountability, for use of money in ways that corrupt the public process, and for lessons we're teaching in how citizens can organize and be effective.

Common Cause, he observed, had taken on everybody – both political parties and industry and labor – and was at the moment in a battle where labor leaders were calling it anti-labor and the Chamber of Commerce was also opposed.

"If Common Cause, dies or goes to sleep tomorrow, people are going to remember it, and, when they lose their grip on their society, say, 'That guy, John Gardner, did something we ought to think about.'

"Citizens action is good for democracy, but it is even better for the citizens. It really gives them a feeling they haven't had in a long time – that America is their venture, theirs to preserve or theirs to neglect, and, through neglect, destroy. If you can't keep that, just forget everything else. Society begins and ends with motivated people and the ideas they have in their heads of what society is or ought to be like."

"The citizens who don't vote, who go around littering their own parks and streets, the workers who are content with low productivity, are all suffering from the same thing. They have forgotten it's their venture. A lot of them have reason to forget because if they try to get into City Council, the door's locked. They can't get in. We're trying to turn that around. We are saying, 'Look, it's your show, and if you ever forget it, nothing will save it.' And that's Common Cause."

Dean Sayre builds Washington Cathedral

"Right now more than any other time in our national history we are adrift spiritually," said the Very Rev. Francis B. Sayre Jr., fifth Dean of the Washington Cathedral. He turned his face toward the study window, and the light fell on the wide-spaced blue eyes, the firm mouth, high cheek bones, and long, stubborn jaw of Woodrow Wilson's grandson. The unmistakable Wilsonian features, and the Dean's moral fervor impress visitors as coming directly down the years from the 28th President. But the Dean's pronouncements from Mount Saint Alban on the nation draw respect not because of his lineage but their vigor.

"I was born in the White House," he said. "I am a real Washingtonian. And grandfather is buried in this Cathedral. I was brought up in Cambridge, Massachusetts, where my father taught law, but we visited grandfather regularly at the S Street house after he left the Presidency."

He does not seek the identification. Indeed, in their childhood he and his brother, tired of being pointed out as Woodrow Wilson's grandsons, decided between them to change their names, and he chose the romantic name of Wolfgang. But, as Wilson once said of himself, a man's rootage is more important than his leafage, and the grandson's origins are plain.

"My last memories of grandfather are after he had his stroke, so he was physically incapacitated to a degree, but his mind was scintillating and sparkling. People see pictures of a crippled old man and they think he was crippled mentally, which was not true; he was very lively and alert, a man of wit and fun, who showed loving care for his grandchildren. I remember a limerick he recited for us. How did it go?

*"As a beauty. I'm not a great star,
There are others more handsome by far.
But my face I don't mind it
Because I'm behind it –
It's the folks in front that I jar.'"*

"There's a curious little human connection between those times and this Cathedral. Often he would take me for an afternoon ride in that old chauffeur-driven Pierce-Arrow. In the back, I remember, was a big fur rug to pull up on a cold day. Once in 1924 we came up here, and he showed me the Cathedral when the only thing standing was just the apse, that one end. When I was called here in 1951 his tomb was in the Bethlehem Chapel, but the intention had been that eventually it would be put in the nave, and in 1956, on the 100th anniversary of his birth, that became my responsibility.

"I was always interested in politics. If my mother didn't notice me, I would sit and listen until 11 o'clock at night to the President and Josephus Daniels and the rest of the entourage. Then in Cambridge my mother was an elector for Al Smith in 1928. She and Mayor Curley campaigned all around Massachusetts, and I argued with violence with my classmates, all of whom were Republican.

"My father taught international law, so our home was filled with foreign students, and then the Harvard Law School sent him as an adviser to the King of Siam. That duty took him around Europe. This made an internationalist out of me from the age of 8. Finally both my parents were deeply religious and tried to share that commitment with their daughter and sons, and, I think, were successfull."

Educated at Williams College, Union Theological Seminary in New York, and Episcopal Theological School at Cambridge, he served as a chaplain

"Gothic is an architecture of whimsy, of inexhaustibility, of mystery. It's never-ending," says the Rev. Francis B. Sayre of the Washington Cathedral.

during World War II, first with the heavy cruiser, USS San Francisco and then as staff chaplain, Philippine Sea Frontier. He married Harriet Hart, daughter of Admiral Thomas C. Hart, Commander-in-Chief of the Asiatic Fleet.

After the war, as rector of St. Paul's Church in East Cleveland, he concentrated on ministry to urban workers, exploring the relation between religion and the industrial society. As Chairman of the United States Committee for Refugees, he was concerned "with the great streams of human dislocation in the world – Arabs, Jews, Chinese, Indians, Tibetans."

Nearly all his life, he said, his interests had been twin – politics and faith – and he had fought the idea "that religion was a private thing to be segregated in one pocket and had no bearing on public life – ethical decisions made by Congress, we'll say – or international affairs. I felt that this was such a narrow view of religion and such a tiny view of God as to be untrue. And, secondly, I have felt that politics was not necessarily a dirty business but, when informed by a deeper level of ethical allegiance, is good. And so my specialty has been the Church and State and their relation."

Didn't that run counter to the historic separation of Church and State?

"The Constitution says that the government shall not favor any religion, but a total separation is not intended, nor would it be right. If our government is totally separate from any ethics, the result is Watergate. If our religion is totally separate from any practical means of carrying out what we believe, it's sterile. I'm saying that they are morally connected but not legally established.

"Many people say they don't want to mix religion and politics. That's because they are threatened by the judgment religion brings to bear on whatever

they're doing. They don't want a challenge that goes against what they conceive to be their immediate welfare. And for that reason, basically, the phrase separation-of-church-and-state has been distorted into meaning an absolute gulf."

Didn't many fear that an involvement of Church with State would produce tyranny?

"And so do I. I detest tyranny in any form, whether it is Hitler or Calvin in Geneva. And I have often said that churchmen should not be entrusted with the affairs of the world, but their moral judgment should be brought to bear upon those who are."

Is he pessimistic?

"I am aware that right now more than at any other time in our national history we are adrift spiritually. All institutions have been challenged by recent events. The Vietnam War had a valid rationale for its inception, but as it went on, that evaporated and we were not flexible enough to acknowledge this. The war became a perfect agony of hypocrisy and evil for our people. What could they believe in? And then on top of that came Watergate and the revelations of immorality of the leadership of our precious nation. It leaves our people in a situation where some superficially attractive forces could appeal to them. So I think we are in a dangerous situation, but I'm not pessimistic ultimately. At bottom within the American people is a reservoir of good will, of humility before the Lord, of neighborliness. Our people may not be actively faithful today. But the residue is there on which could be built a new faith in a new shape."

What is a cathedral built for?

Dozens of purposes, but primarily it bears a witness in the public life at the place where decisions are made about that life. That's real job. It's the role of Notre Dame in Paris. It was symbolic of the coming together of the Franks, the Goths, and the Visigoths, who first made a

nation and then threw up Notre Dame in the year 1000 to be an emblem of this compact of people in a common faith. Well, that's what this is. That's why so many churches use it. Where do you have a state funeral? Ike's was here. Harry Truman's was here. Earl Warren's was here because the state needs a place at a time like that to say we are one people under God.

"In 1893 there were romantics who thought, 'Paris and London have cathedrals and Washington ought to have one.' They made no provision as to how it would be financed, built or run. They left all that to those who followed. They bought a piece of ground down there in the city and in 1898 chose a bishop of vision, Henry Yates Satterlee. He said, 'We will build instead on the highest point in the city and if we can't do it perfectly, as fine as man can do it, we won't do it at all. We will skimp on nothing.' And that has been adhered to. That's why it's so slow. Now there's a witness of excellence in an era that skimps and cheats and shortcuts.

"Gothic is an architecture of whimsy, of inexhaustibility, of mystery. It's never-ending. You can keep on adding to it. You don't say it in words in the Gothic. You say it with a little carving, a tiny stained glass window. The ideal of Gothic is, of course, like a tree, you know, rooted deep in the earth, the great fluted trunks lifting their branches up to the sky, and the bosses that are carved up there, the little keystones, are fruit and leaves. The trunks spread their branches to heaven. Well now, this society, it kills the tree. It wrecks the earth. It thumbs its nose at heaven. How eloquent then is this Gothic tree? Built to last a thousand years."

The Dean looked up at the west facade blurred by the web of scaffolding, a gigantic crane extending its arm over the entrance. "A cathedral," he said, "is never finished."

Washington Cathedral towers over tea party

The Cathedral Church of Saint Peter and Saint Paul at Mount Saint Alban is the scene of many community activities. The Cathedral looms on the highest point of land in the District of Columbia. The Gloria in Excelsis Tower soars 301 feet. The nave will be completed in 1976, and the nation's Bicentennial will be celebrated with a year-long series of special services, musical performances, and gala events in the Cathedral.

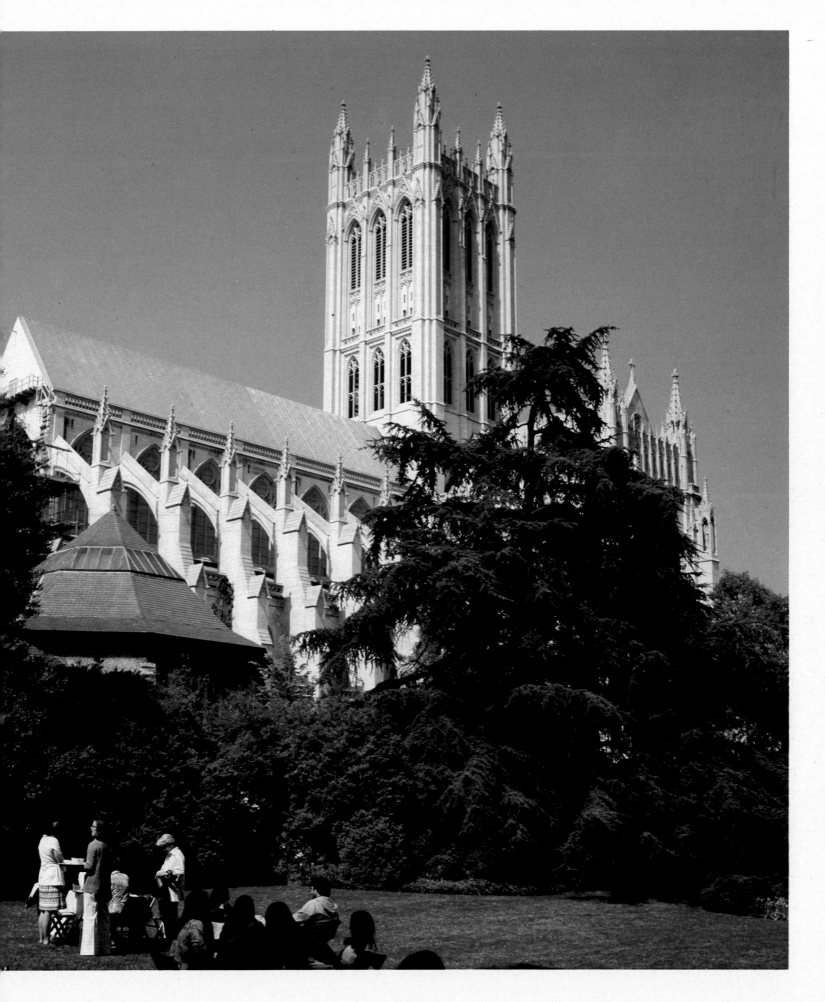

Work goes on at Cathedral during fair

Even as Washingtonians enjoy a fair in the Cathedral close, workmen, at left, haul slabs for construction. Begun in 1906, the main structure will be finished by 1984 with the completion of the St. Peter and St. Paul towers at the west end. Among the six largest in the world, it covers 83,012 feet. Height of nave is 104 feet and the span is 41 feet. It is 518 feet in length. The massive central pillars are 27 feet in diameter and reach 39 feet below the nave floor.

Churches find national homes in Washington

Washington is the site for more than 20 national churches. St. John's, far left, "the Church of the Presidents," is in Lafayette Park opposite the White House. Pew 54 is reserved for the Presidents. All since James

Madison have attended services, many as members. The Islamic Center, upper center, raises a slender minaret, capped with Islam's crescent moon, over Rock Creek Park. It houses magnificent examples of Moslem art and culture: a pulpit of 10,000 fitted pieces of wood, rich Iranian prayer rugs, and lovely Turkish tiles. The National Shrine of the Immaculate Conception, lower center, the largest Catholic Church in America, has a 329-foot bell tower, and 200 stained glass windows. The Washington Temple, world's largest Latter-Day Saint Temple, looms above I-495. Topping the eastern spire is a statue to angel Moroni.

National Aboretum woodland and Rock Creek Park offer room to relax

Youthful couple, above, Diane and Michael Jones, feed ducks in National Aboretum. Other sightseers walk woodland trails bright with dogwood and ablaze with azaleas. Covering 415 scenic acres in Mount Hamilton section, the fine gardens feature a fern valley, and a hillside of dwarf conifers, a slope of camellias and 250 kinds of crabapples.

*Families, above, enjoy
a cookout in
Rock Creek Park. At left,
a couple strolls
through the National
Arboretum. Congress au-
thorized devel-
opment of the outdoor
museum in 1927
for research, education,
and pure pleasure.
Seasonal highlights offer
a year-round show.
Fall features spectacular
displays in a natural
forest of yellow hickories
and tulip poplars and
red gums and dogwood.*

Buildings offer contrasts in style and size

The Willard Hotel, a mellow old party, above, stands on Pennsylvania Avenue. Civic organizations are striving to save it from the wrecker's ball. Most critics consider the Rayburn Office Building, right, to be beyond redemption. Completed in 1965 for House offices, it cost $100 million and is one of the largest of its kind. It also is widely regarded as one of the least attractive. The small fountain in the nearby Botanical Gardens adds a much-needed note of grace to the mass.

The passing scene in Georgetown is always vivid

Just off Wisconsin Avenue an artist finds space for a sidewalk studio. The models and scenery are endless. The community or town or state of mind that is Georgetown manages to contain, if not blend, many elements. It is the refuge of the government executive, the old, native Washingtonian, footloose youths, office holders and seekers, Democrats and Republicans, black and white, rich, poor and middle-class. No wonder tourists haunt Georgetown.

58

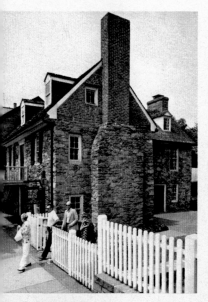

The Old Stone House, below, stands at 3051 M Street. Christopher. Layhman, a cabinet-maker, built it in 1765, 14 years after the town was founded. He used the front downstairs room as his shop. It is the only pre-Revolutionary house in Georgetown.

Street vendors, shoppers, and sightseers, throng Georgetown's Wisconsin Avenue, above. Periodically, officials try, without lasting success, to drive away the vendors. They come back.

Georgetown became a haven for the younger generation during the 1960s when Maryland and Virginia imposed stricter regulations on minors than did the District of Columbia.

That Congress set the park aside is a miracle. It began pondering the possibility in 1866. Early-day environmentalists pleaded first that it should be saved for itself, then for promoting real estate values, and, finally, to protect Rock Creek from sewage. On September 27, 1890 Congress acted. It authorized the acquisition of the Rock Creek Valley as a "pleasuring ground for the benefit and enjoyment of the people of the United States."

An even greater miracle will occur if Congress and Montgomery County act to protect the watershed that feeds Rock Creek in the north.

Picturesque individuals, as well as animals, have found refuge there. Teddy Roosevelt led his band of children, as well as puffing politicians, through the Park. Old Harry Byrd used to leave the Mayflower Hotel, slide under a fence, and take a long walk before breakfast. Bicyclists, joggers, horseback riders, and picnickers recuperate in its green depths.

Such a hold do the Washington Redskins have on Washington's allegiance that they seem to be aborigines of the Potomac, but until 1937 they were the Braves of Boston. Among Redskin traditions is quarterback Sonny Jurgensen, who was, until the spring of 1964, a Philadelphia Eagle; but a decade is an eon in football. In the autumn, with the red leaves, come bumper stickers proclaiming: I ROOT FOR THE REDSKINS AND I LIKE SONNY.

On Georgetown University's field, the 40-year-old Sonny was throwing footballs to much larger, younger men, spiraling the pigskin 30 yards flawlessly, so that, as one by one, the men ran down the field, the ball arched through the sultry July air and plopped into their hands.

Jurgensen, was born in Wilmington, N.C., and, after starring at Duke University, began playing professional football when some of the men to whom he was throwing were in cribs. He lives with his family in a house near Mount Vernon, home of George Washington.

The National Football League players were on strike, but the Redskins in shorts and T-shirts were working out without coaches. Red-headed, squarish, Jurgensen looked like a slightly pot-bellied and aging Apollo as he flung footballs in the air as fast as they were handed to him, so that they rained, thick as coconuts, into the hands of the pounding, panting giants. Finishing, Jurgensen threw the last one from behind his back and it rose as stylishly and fell as unerringly on target.

Walking to the gymnasium he said he regretted that injuries and operations had prevented his making a full contribution for three years. "Football is a difficult game to play healthy, and when you're half healthy, it's impossible to play," he said. "I still love the game, and I feel I can help the Redskins. I'd like to be a part of bringing the championship and Super Bowl to Washington.

Charming townhouses line Georgetown's streets. Pictured at the top of the page is Cox's Row, five brick houses built in 1790 in the Federal style on the north side of N Street. Their proud builder, Colonel John Cox, was the first elected (1823) Mayor of Georgetown.

A bronze figure of John Carroll, the founder of Georgetown University in 1789, broods near the school's main gate. Behind him loom the gray, Victorian Gothic towers of the old Healy Building. Carroll was the first American bishop and first Archbishop of Baltimore.

Georgetown University, directed by Jesuits, is the oldest Catholic institution of higher education in the United States. It also is the oldest University in Washington. Many American diplomats have been graduated from its School of Foreign Service, which was founded in 1919.

Georgetown University adds to ferment

The people have been great to me. They supported us when we were losing."

What did he enjoy about football?

"I been doing it all my life."

That week his mother had sent him a snapshot, taken at the age of 6, in which, preparing to throw, he was turning the ball in his hands, feeling for the seam.

What meant the most now to him?

"Winning," he said. "I have no individual records to set. The important thing is to do your part in a 40-man effort."

Had he decided when to retire?

"No, I haven't. It's a week-to-week thing with me," said the 40-year-old.

Two suburban communities within Washington's embrace – Alexandria and Georgetown – preceded it in history, both founded by Scotch merchants. Two others – Reston and Columbia – issued full-grown in the last half of the 20th century, instant towns with conveniences and vistas.

Georgetown, which began to take shape in the 1700s, now ranges from Rock Creek Park to Georgetown University and from the Potomac River to Dumbarton Oaks. There's an atmosphere of the small town and another time in cobblestone, tree-shaded streets and deep, secret gardens in the rear of elegant townhouses and in the way residents chat casually with storekeepers. There also is an air of the carnival along the lower portion of Wisconsin Avenue, thronged with street vendors of junk jewelry, books, pots, and what not. The strip came into being in the 1960s when Maryland and Virginia laws regulated minors more strictly than did Washington's. Now Georgetown is a mecca for youths and tourists come to look at youths. Here, anyway, generation, economic and racial gaps are bridged. In most of the shoe stores the clientele is young and black. It is an interesting paradox that while the offspring of affluent Americans are shucking their shoes in favor of sandals or bare feet, sons and daughters from low-income homes are buying ever more fashionable footwear.

Georgetown, for all its seeming to stay the same, is accustomed to change. The advent of railroads and steamships spelled an end to its bustling port. Now its C. & O. Canal is an environmentalist's delight for bikes and hikes. After the Civil War much of Georgetown lapsed into slums, to be roused and restored by Franklin Roosevelt's New Dealers. Georgetown University contributes to the heady, intellectual atmosphere of daily emigres from government.

Alexandrians are not of Egyptian origin despite the frowning tower, patterned on the Pharos lighthouse at Alexandria Egypt, that rises 400 feet on Shooters Hill, a site once proposed for the Capitol. That is the Masonic National Memorial to George Washington, and it contains picturesque memora-

City markets offer the best of everything

In old Eastern Market on Capitol Hill, shoppers, below and upper right, browse amid the choicest viands. The city owns the market on Seventh Street, where neighbors meet, chat, and eat. Another festive place is the seafood market on Main Street, east of 14th Street Bridge, nestled between 1-95 and marina.

When the District Sub-committee tried to abolish the seafood market as unsightly, Virginia and Maryland Congressmen arose. Tom Downing said, "I think it's pictures-que, and, further, offers Washington fresh fish: perch, herring, rock, flounder, blue, shad, mullet, spot, trout, croaker, snapper, catfish, porgie and bass."

Alexandrians re-enact the adoption on July 18, 1774 of the Fairfax Resolves, a vital statement of human rights penned by George Mason of Gunston Hall. In Gadsby's Tavern, above, actor in white wig portrays George Washington, who presided at the meeting. At left, Mason and Washington emerge from the tavern. Costumed residents parade and stand guard. Alexandria's cup runneth over with history. George Washington used Gadsby's as headquarters while a lieutenant colonel in the Virginia Militia, and from the tavern's steps reviewed his troops for the last time, ending where he had begun.

Alexandria steps
out front celebrating
Bicentennial

bilia, including the clock that was stopped at the time of his death. By night, from the air, the flood-lit pyramid looks like a golden, molten candlestick.

Alexandria bills itself rightly as George Washington's home town. He surveyed it as a youth and accepted his first military command there. In 1974, a step ahead of the rest of the nation, Alexandria commemorated the bicentennial of the signing of the Fairfax Resolves, Virginia's support of the Boston Tea Party. George Mason wrote them, and George Washington presided at the meeting that adopted them.

The town is named for John Alexander, a Scot who would sell his land only if it took his name. In the Ramsey House Information Center, formerly the home of Alexandria's first Mayor, Peg Sinclair, information director, observed that Alexandria's seaport once vied with New York. "Thank goodness we lost," she said, "or we wouldn't have all this." The town has 1,000 18th and 19th century buildings. Ships bringing newsprint to Washington's newspapers still dock at Alexandria, and a training destroyer is home-ported there.

Newcomers, once settled, become confirmed Alexandrians, ready to rush to City Hall to turn back modernity.

Near Alexandria off I-95 at Lorton is Gunston Hall, "elegant little house" of George Mason, a framer of the Republic who wrote the Virginia Declaration of Rights, the foundation for the Federal Constitution's Bill of Rights.

Mason usually is an afterthought in history texts, which wouldn't bother him. His concern at a Colonial convention was to do the job right, with as little haranguing as possible, and return to his wife, the former Ann Eilbeck of Maryland, and their plantation next door to Mount Vernon. But Revolutionary leaders cherished him as their elder statesman – he was seven years older than his neighbor, George Washington – and kept pulling him into the political arena.

He was gray-eyed, stocky, straight-backed, a wedge of a man. When the Federal Constitutional Convention, meeting in Philadelphia, declined to outlaw slavery or adopt a Bill of Rights, Mason refused to sign the Constitution. At last, years later, he had his way partly when James Madison introduced in Congress the first 10 amendments comprising the Constitution's Bill of Rights.

Gunston Hall's modest appearance, like that of the builder, is deceptive. The upper story's six bedrooms housed nine offspring. And the master joiner who saw to the interior was gifted William Buckland, whom Mason brought from London under a four-year bill of indenture. When Buckland finished in three, a pleased Mason let him out a year early.

When Ann died, Mason said, "She never met me without a smile." He wore mourning the rest

A marina near Alexandria draws a sailor, right, and spectators, below. The city once vied with New York as a port, but now harbors commuters working in D.C. Across the Potomac stand the cliffs of Crystal City, a complex of offices and residences so complete that the inhabitants, if they so choose, need never venture out.

Cobblestoned streets and more than 1,000 18th and 19th century buildings give Alexandria an air of antiquity. Many artifacts are displayed in the George Washington Bicentennial Center and Museum. The area also has sizeable wetlands and a bike trail that leads along the Potomac River by woods to Mount Vernon.

Alexandrians enjoy view of pleasure boats on Potomac

George Mason's Gunston Hall, left, is close to Alexandria at Lorton off I-95. On display is the tiny table on which Mason wrote Virginia's Declaration of Rights. In his elegant garden, walks thread green boxwood taller than six feet and stretch 200 feet to a lookout over a deer park and the blue Potomac. Eagles nest nearby. The Ramsey House, below, the fine home of Alexandria's first Mayor, is now the town's information center. At right, the panorama of Alexandria's King Street is dominated by the Masonic National Memorial to President George Washington. Tower of pink granite is patterned on the Pharos lighthouse at Alexandria, Egypt.

Memorial to Washington looms over Alexandria

69

of his life. Seven years after Ann's death he married Sarah Brent, 50, a friend of the family of "amiable and domestic character," who helped rear Ann's brood. Gunston Hall's reception center is named for Ann. Somewhere there ought to be a remembrance of Sarah.

A week before Mason died, Thomas Jefferson visited him and the two talked over the old, glorious days when their necks were near the British noose. Jefferson's presence in the house may be gathered from a gift to his old friend, a library ladder that folds into a pole. Jefferson, good at summing things up, called George Mason "the wisest man of his generation."

Reston, named for its founder, Robert Simon, was the first major effort in the United States to create at one stroke a full-scale, self-contained city on the perimeter of a huge urban center. That it was successful is demonstrated by the rise in the resident population from 500 in 1965 to 20,000 in 1972. In Simon's seven goals for Reston the first was to make available the widest choice of opportunities for full use of leisure time. Entering the town's first unit, Lake Anne Village, with the 15-story Heron House rising above 30-acre Lake Anne, the immediate feeling is of coming upon an Old World festival or a new World's Fair.

To plan Columbia in Maryland, Rouse Company first impaneled 14 authories and let them swap ideas at a series of two-day meetings on optimums for education, health, transportation, and recreation. Then basing each neighborhood around a small elementary school, the company constructed three neighborhoods for each village and seven villages around a downtown of commercial buildings. The response was nearly as instantaneous as the town. Opened in 1967, Columbia had a population of 34,000 by 1974 and looked to a goal of 110,000.

Washington has two splendid airports. Dulles International, poised like a wing in Virginia's green Loudoun County, is closer to Washington than are Kennedy and LaGuardia Airports to New York. Dulles induces composure. There are no long walks down mud-dauber tunnels from field to terminal. Instead one rides, cushioned, in gigantic, rubber-tired mobile lounges with interiors that look, reassuringly, like ferry boats. Under the terminal's great awning, the soft, beige light is restful. Dulles, said architect Eero Saarinen, "is the best thing I've done."

National Airport is located on the capital's doormat. Planes are a fixture over West Potomac Park. At night, coming in low, blinking red and yellow wing-lights, a plane seems to hang in the sky, a new constellation.

National is the scene of hairy, harried departures for commuters from Washington to New York, the world's political and financial headquarters. National's help is geared to personal emergencies.

A tardy, would-be passenger stumbles rumpled and wall-eyed into the terminal where a roving clerk, sensing his destination, steers him straight to Gate 10. Tall, relaxed Jim Timberblake waits calmly while the latecomer fumbles for fare. Outside jets whine. The nostalgic fragrance of kerosene oil fills the air.

"You don't seem tense," observes the passenger.

"I started to take a nap while you were writing the check," says Timberlake, closing his eyes and dropping his head to one side.

"Call him Mr. Cool," says the other clerk.

In the plane the passengers, middle-aged and brief-cased, seem encapsulated, packaged for shipment like so many eggs, to be shot to New York. Mary Robertson the stewardess – blonde, freckled, open-faced – says you can spot the Washington-New York commuters on the airport's ramps. They require special, tender care. Say something to them, and their lips move soundlessly. They're looking to a hard day's work, thinking about the trip by limousine into the city and back again. Ready for work, they tune out everything else. Airborne, they take out briefcases, and, all along the length of the plane, heads lean across the aisle to confer, hands pass papers back and forth. Already they are at work.

No story that the airport's cab drivers hear is any more interesting than their own. There is William Rearden, who came to Washington from Greenville, S.C. shortly after Franklin Roosevelt.

"In the whole year of 1936, working on the farm from can't to can't – 'can't see when you get up, can't see when you go to bed' – I cleared $34. So I told my daddy I was going to Washington. Congressman Taylor of Greenville helped me get a job at Archives and I worked there 24 years and then took a job with circulation at the Washington Post. My wife and I have a son stationed at the Pentagon, and I'm pretty proud of myself. In 40 years here and 22 in South Carolina, I've never been" – he held up a thumb and forefinger tightly closed – "in that much trouble."

Washington's pull continues. Nearly 20 per cent of its cab drivers are from Africa, attending Howard University, preparing for careers at home. They seem to share a national trait, a mixture of merriment and fortitude. A youth from Nigeria, studying to be an architect, has not seen his wife and two children for two years.

"Washington is quite a nice city with lots of opportunities," he said, "but one needs lots of determination and courage."

Only 15 miles from the White House on the George Washington Parkway are the Great Falls of the Potomac, a cataract that plunges 77 feet in less than three quarters of a mile and winds out of sight between the sheer rock sides of rugged Mather George. Sightseers may follow trails through 800 acres of woods.

"Instant city" of Reston is prospering

Residents of Reston in Northern Virginia enjoy sailing on cool Lake Anne and strolling in the town plaza. Reston, near Washington, is the country's first totally planned town on the perimeter of a major city. Some 45 percent of the space is supposed to be reserved for public purposes. Opened in 1967, Reston expects to have a population of 75,000 persons by 1980.

Dulles International, the
first commercial
airport designed for jets
from the start,
was an aesthetic success
from its dedica-
tion in November, 1962
in Loudoun County
Virginia. It has proven
a financial one
as well. New Reston, left,
affords many such
amenities as a lake for
boats downtown.

Dulles, new
towns, brighten
suburbs

Columbia, right, a bedroom
community to both
Baltimore and Washington,
has, furthermore,
a sizeable portion of population, at least
30 per cent, that says put.

73

Built for $ 77 million in 1966, the Watergate complex of hotel and apartments is one of the city's prestigious addresses. Neighbor to the Kennedy Center, just a stroll from the White House, it drew Republicans and the Democratic National Committee headquarters. On June 17, 1972 a break-in at the Committee office, detected by a Watergate guard, started a chain of events that finally culminated in the resignation of President Richard Nixon.

Round on round the Watergate complex rises above the Potomac River

Off George Washington Parkway 15 miles from the White House, the Potomac River races through Great Fall

...scading over huge rocks, and, dropping 77 feet in less than three-quarters of a mile, plunger into Mather George.

Theodore Reed, director of the National Zoological Park, thrusts hunk of bread into hungry elephant's mouth. African variety has low forehead and ears shaped like Africa.

The birds and beasts were there... at the Zoo

Sleek California sea lions perform, above, for appreciative audience. In the flight toom of the bird house, nothing separates the birds from the visitors. At right, a bright bird and sightseers size up each other. To step into the room is to enter a lush green, man-made jungle.

Reached by a bridge from the bird house is the flight cage, above, six arches of steel covered with netting of vinyl-coated wire enclosing a circle 130 feet in diameter. One of the rarest animals in the zoo is the Indian rhinoceros. Less than 400 are left in the world.

The female Indian rhino, at left, relaxes in pool with her offspring. The ponderous male weighs four tons. The one-horned rhino inhabits marshy plains of Northern India, Assam, and Nepal, where they have runways through 15-foot high grass to their favorite waterholes.

Pandas feast on willows in National Zoo

Ling-Ling and Hsing-Hsing, presented by the People's Republic of China to President and Mrs. Nixon in 1972 for the people of the United States, have become the most popular animals in the zoo. Born in the mountains of Central China, they grow to weigh 300 pounds, and honk and bleat for sounds.

Man has lent a hand in shaping some natural wonders in Washington. To step into the bulbous-roofed Botanical Gardens at the foot of the Capitol is to be transported to a banana republic. The U.S. National Arboretum covers 415 acres in the Mount Hamilton section of Washington. Its varied sections include a hillside blazing with 70,000 azaleas, a fern forest, 700 kinds of holly, and an assemblage of dwarf and slow-growing conifers. In the Kenilworth Aquatic Gardens, next to the Anacostia estuary in the city's eastern corner, are 11 acres of ponds planted with water-lillies and lotuses in which lurk six species of turtles, including snapper.

The National Zoological Park – the official U.S. zoo – opened in 1889 in Rock Creek Park with a few animals that had accumulated at the Smithsonian Institution on the Mall. It has grown into one of the world's best and one of the last major free zoos. "The taxpayers deserve something for their money," said Dr. Theodore Reed, its director.

Of more than 3,000 animals and 900 species – golden-maned lions, blue-eyed white tigers, ear-flapping, trunk waving elephants, sleek and sinuous sea lions, four-ton slabsided rhinos looking like rusting boilers, the most popular is a roly poly pair of pandas, gifts in 1972 from the People's Republic of China to the people of the United States, the most tangible evidence yet of detente.

Weighing about 300 pounds, they look like cuddly black and white bears, but, said Dr. Reed, they are neither bears nor raccoons, just pandas. Being large and largely vegetarians, they don't have enemies. To grind bamboo, the panda's back teeth have been modified into molars similar to those in horses and cows. The jaw muscles have enlarged, and the brow over the eyes, to which they are attached, has extended outward, which gives the panda its round, clownish face.

The wrist bone has extended an inch and a half, and, covered by a fleshy pad, functions as a thumb, giving the panda a dexterity surpassed only by humans and apes. It is as if the panda eats with mittens, picking bamboo stalks from a tub and pulling them through its mouth to strip off the leaves. About 90 Washingtonians are growing bamboo in their backyards, and every morning a truck goes out from the zoo for a fresh supply.

They have only four calls: a honk, a blat, a buzz, and a squeal. Life, among pandas, is one long Halloween. They are cold-weather creatures and love the snow.

"One winter," said Dr. Reed, "we built snowmen for them. Ling-Ling, the female, demolished her snowman, and thoroughly enjoyed doing it. The last thing she did was pick up the head and throw it in the water pool. Hsing-Hsing climbed up his snowman, grabbed the carrot-nose off, and ran away and ate it."

Washington on Saturday presents contrasting scenes of work, play

In a northwest neighborhood a group of friends, left, take it easy. Elsewhere, there is work to do. The Rev. Gordon Cosby, pastor of the Church of the Savior, right, pauses with some members in their drive to renovate and restore buildings and lives in the inner city. The work crew, left to right, is Evelyn Boston, Terry Flood, Carolyn Cresswell, and Janet Colwell. Every Saturday the members repair another room in their effort to make Washington more livable.

The ecumenical Church of the Savior, with headquarters near DuPont Circle, has organized a nonprofit corporation, Jubilee Housing, to renovate the city block by block. As the members repair rooms, they also build communities by teaching reading, helping find jobs, placing children in foster homes, operating a day camp, child care centers, and coffee house.

83

Buses crowd Washington's busy K Street

Washington is a highly mobile city, always on the go, as is evident in a look along K Street, a main commercial thoroughfare between Georgetown and the city's downtown. Lining curbs on both sides of the busy street and pulling into center lanes are often as many as two dozen buses. Relief is on the way via Metro, a modern subway system.

Rush hour traffic keeps D.C. policeman alert. His task will be eased with completion in 1985 of the Washington Area Metropolitan Transit Authority's subway system. Costing $ 3 billion, the 98-mile network will pull the downtown and Maryland and Virginia suburbs together.

Pandas apparently are in no danger of becoming extinct. They have all the food they desire at arm's length, and the Chinese seem to regard the panda as the benign old man of the forest. "The historically amicable relationship probably goes back to Confucius and Buddhas and their focus on the peaceful, meditative life," suggested Dr. Reed. "I suspect that the panda's survival has something to do with his lifestyle fitting the contemplative turn of the Chinese. The animal has quit the rat race of the prey-predator relationship and just eats bamboo and lets the world go by."

A woman who had been observing the pandas planted herself in front of the zoo director and declared: "You take care of our pandas, you hear?"

"Thank you, ma'am, and the rest of the animals, too," replied Dr. Reed.

With the vacancy rate on Washington dwellings at less than 1 per cent, the city's housing need is acute. Members of the ecumenical Church of the Savior, led by the Rev. Gordon Cosby, have set out to rehabilitate Washington room by room, block by block. If that seems Quixotic, then their drive for low-income housing was moving when impounded funds stalled Federal programs.

The church has headquarters at 2025 Massachusetts Avenue, but no large sanctuary. The members consider the community their place of work and worship. Incorporated as Jubilee Housing, they bought two apartment buildings in the Adams-Morgan area and began negotiating for two more in the same block.

Found painting a wall in a third-floor apartment, the minister explained, still applying the brush, "We renovate the apartment while the people are living here. They simply are out for the day, and when they return, this room will be done and next time we'll do another."

The housing effort, he said, is only one facet. Other groups are teaching reading, placing children in foster homes, aiding the elderly, running a coffeehouse, scheduling health testing programs, jobhunting for applicants, operating a day camp for 200 children, and raising sod for sale to Washington Stadium to help finance the multiple ventures.

"You see, our strategy is to focus on a very small area," said Dr. Cosby. "In these two buildings are 90 families. In two more on the same block are an additional 42 units. We are trying to come to know them through apartment management and to get them to trust us and one another to the point of building a community.

"We're concentrating on one city block so that all the services begin to impact on one another and something really starts to happen to the quality of the people's lives. Then we hope to work with these tenants as they begin to make the same effort in another city block, so that we start renewing the city of Washington.

"Three other congregations are working with us, and we hope to bring in many more because we are concerned with the total housing picture in Washington."

Dr. Cosby devised the approach while he was a chaplain during World War II with the 101st Airborne Division. "There was no way in the world to minister to 3,000 soldiers over miles of combat zone, so in each of the 12 companies I organized a small spiritual nucleus," he said.

After the war he decided his place was among the urban poor.

Two of his brothers are working in urban ministries in Lynchburg, Virginia. "The fourth brother," he said, "is carrying on the family business, and my father used to say that if one more of his sons entered the seminary he was going to the cemetery."

Among church members working in the apartment was Evelyn Boston. "If you just start off with the housing effort," she said, "it does so much for someone to have a decent place to live."

Another worker, Terry Flood, and her husband are acting as a support family in counseling an inner city family how to manage finances in buying a house with the church's help.

"They simply never have had the responsibility of a house," she explained, "Someone has to point out that if they want a backyard cemented, they must decide whether they need that or a new hot water heater or a paint job for the kitchen."

Carolyn Cresswell, a young realtor whose husband is a medical student, located the two apartments. "One city department found over 5,000 violations that we had to tend to within 30 days," she said, "and 90 volunteers from the Army Corps of Engineers came the first Saturday and shoveled stuff out of the basement.

"We had considered seeking help from Housing and Urban Development, but the first thing it requires is that you totally renovate the project. To get Federal money, we would have had to move everybody out – and there is no place, literally no place, for everybody to go. And under HUD requirements you can't simply repair an elevator, you have to replace it. You can't just mend plumbing, you must replace it. On this building HUD set a required expenditure of $11,000 per unit. We can do those things for about $1,000 per unit and put the difference into other services. And then, too, we have the opportunity to learn to know the people.

"You come into this apartment today and work on one room and you come back next Saturday and work on the next and by the time you've been here five or six weeks, you and the family know each other, and there's a good relationship. If you just moved them into a totally new apartment, you would miss that. We figure we're miles ahead for doing it this long way."

The People's Capitol

Like the legislative body it houses, the United States Capitol is in some details quirky, wasteful of space, and ostentatious, but always grand and imposing. It appears as much a work of nature as a work of art, and a critic might as well object to extraneous features in the contours of the Grand Canyon or question a turn in the sweeping course of Niagara Falls as suggest that an ornament is out of order on the Capitol's vast white cliffs and noble summit. It is confirmation in rock that the whole is greater than the sum of the parts.

To the American people the Capitol is a never ending source of interest and confidence both as a structure and as the engine of government, mighty and yet exquisitely balanced and attuned to differences. It is theirs and they love it.

Their estimate matches Thomas Jefferson's. He said that the original plan "captivated the eyes and judgement of all . . . It is simple, noble, beautiful, and excellently distributed, and moderate in size."

No longer moderate in size, the Capitol expanded far beyond the original design – the low dome flanked by two wings – of Dr. William Thornton. Jefferson, while astounded, probably would be pleased at the harmonious changes. The Capitol simply has grown with the country.

Dr. Thornton – physician, inventor, painter – was Jeffersonian in his varied interests and ability to do a thing when the idea struck him. Learning there was a prize of $500 and a city lot for a design of the Capitol, he wrote from his home in the West Indies for permission to compete. The deadline was three months past, but the judges hadn't liked any of the entries, and so they agreed. Studying architecture as he went along, he drew the plans. Jefferson who devised the competition, specified a Greek classic design, but to imagine its four-stage dome, girded with columns, rising anywhere but Jenkins Hill is impossible. It seems as indigenous as the carvings of corn cobs and tobacco leaves with which Benjamin Latrobe, the second architect, decked caps of columns throughout the interior.

Latrobe restored the Capitol that had been burned by the British in the War of 1812. Eight years later Charles Bulfinch completed and crowned the link between the two wings. Congress authorized two additions in 1850, and Thomas U. Walter replaced the wooden dome with one of cast-iron. It is composed of two shells, one imposed upon the other, that expand and contract with the temperature. Weighing 8,909,200 pounds, rising 284 feet above the East Plaza, it is an engineering tour de force. In 1955 Congress approved Speaker Sam Rayburn's proposal for a 33½ foot eastern extension of the central portion, which was completed in time for President Kennedy's Inauguration on January 20, 1961.

With a mountain's immensity, the Capitol seems able to absorb most alterations without changing its basic bulk or profile. Those that intrude come to be accepted, even cherished, as foibles in a loved one. The statue of Freedom atop the Capitol dome looks, startlingly, as if some huge bird had lit on its head. Sculptor Thomas Crawford designed the bronze figure with the soft cap of freed Roman slaves, but Jefferson Davis, the Secretary of War in charge of the construction, objected to the cap as offensive to the South, and Crawford substituted a crest of eagle head and feathers. Freedom, some say, looks like the Indian princess Pocahontas.

Covering 16½ acres, extending 751 feet in length and 350 feet in width, the Capitol is a landscape that alters subtly in changing lights and seasons. The East Front is the scene of action. The West Front's role is that of a symbol, looking out serenely over Washington and the nation.

West Front of Capitol overlooks city

Washington's main streets radiate like spokes in a wheel from the majestic Capitol; and the deeds of Congress radiate through laws and appropriations into every community in America. The nation's life revolves around the Capitol's democratic hub.

In the soft light of a summer evening, after the air has been freshened with a shower, the Capitol, dreaming, has the wavery, insubstantial quality of an Impressionistic painting. On a crisp wintry morning, its lines are hard-edged as the light clarifies and even seems to magnify details along the magnificent white facade.

The East Front catches most of a day's traffic. And a platform built above the steps before the central East Portico has been the site of Presidential Inaugurations since Andrew Jackson brought the ceremony out to people in 1829. An Inauguration is a kind of synopsis in a sprawling, continuing, improbable novel in which all the threads of plot and cast of characters are brought together every four years. The sense of a review is all the stronger now that the national family can look in on television.

And television's gadgetry, which is not on view to the family, occupies what looks like an enormous five-story cash register on stilts facing the Inaugural stands.

The Capitol looks like a wedding cake, with guards standing here and there on the dome's towering tiers, toy soldiers placed by a child.

What a parade has crossed the East Portico: Jackson, with bold nose and flaring cloak, the Republic's eagle; Lincoln at his Second Inaugural, war-worn but "with malice toward none, with charity for all," drawing compassion from an inexhaustible well; Teddy Roosevelt, walking not softly but crashing through bureaucracies' brush, brandishing the big stick; Franklin Roosevelt, voice lilting, proclaiming "nothing to fear but fear itself;" Truman and his supreme matter-of-factness, dismissing polls after his 1948 upset victory as "sleeping pills" to the electorate; Eisenhower and the wonderfully earnest expression that occasionally beclouded his face, to be broken by the sunny, disarming grin, a grandfather to fix the world's skinned knee; Johnson, his silver-streaked hair like lines running in an old stump, hungry for history's confirmation; Nixon, gesticulating, advocating, preparing to open gaps in the walls between America and Asia.

The incident-filled Kennedy Inauguration: the capital snow-draped as by a sloppy pastry cook; the Capitol dome, freshly painted, gleaming ivory in the cold; the Cardinal praying into eternity until the rostrum's heater fired up in protest; Robert Frost reading "The Gift Outright," about giving ourselves to the land, and, poetry at the service of power, changing a word in the last line at Kennedy's request from conditional "would" to affirmative "will"; the sun's dancing in the old man's eyes, and Vice President Johnson, power at the service of poetry, holding his cowboy hat as a shield; the young President, shoulders hunched, fledgling-like, chin high, urging, "Ask not what your country . . . ask what you . . .," and all through

Figures from history throng Statuary Hall

Statues of the states' most distinguished sons stare at one another across vast Statuary Hall, where formerly the members of the House engaged in fierce debate. The House moved to new quarters in 1857 and set aside the old Hall as a Valhalla in 1864. Preparing to rise in debate, left,

is Wisconsin's Robert M.
La Follette Sr.
Other likenesses in the
row are of Lou-
isiana's Huey Long,
Nebraska's
William Jennings Bryan,
Tennessee's John
Sevier, and West Vir-
ginia's Francis
H. Pierpont. At right,
arms folded, is
Vermont's Ethan Allen.

Ethan demanded the sur-
render of Fort Ticon-
deroga in the name of the
Continental Congress
and the Great Jehovah!
South Carolina's
John C. Calhoun, hands on
hips, is next,
followed by Michigan's
Lewis Cass,
holding crumpled prepared
text, and Dela-
ware's Caesar Rodney.

Rotunda's eye shows allegory of Washington

A fresco, "The Apotheosis of Washington," fills the dome's eye and shows Washington with allegorical figures. Artist Brumidi, an Italian immigrant, spent 25 years decorating the Capitol. The frieze rimming the Rotunda was begun by Brumidi, continued by his pupil, Filippo Castaggini, and finished in 1957 by Allyn Cox. Three portraits of Washington hang in the Capitol. The one by Gilbert Stuart, above, is the Vaughan-Sinclair portrait in the National Gallery of Art.

the stands, one after another, a bouffant hairdo. On entering the Rotunda, the great cylindrical hall 187 feet high and 97 feet across, the visitor peers into the dome as into the lavishly decorated interior of an Easter Egg. In the dome's eye, done in fresco colors of a rosy-hued sunset, is the "Apotheosis of George Washington," the Father of His Country attended by allegorical figures. It is the work of Constantino Brumidi, a refugee in 1852 from Italy, who vowed to "make beautiful the Capitol of the one country on earth in which there is liberty." He was doing a frieze of the nation's history around the dome's rim when he slipped and dangled in the air 15 minutes. The shock hastened his death a few months later.

Around the Rotunda's walls are magnificent paintings of the Revolutionary War: the Declaration of Independence, the surrender of Lord Cornwallis, the surrender of General Burgoyne at Saratoga, and George Washington resigning his commission. The artist, John Turnbull, was an aide-de-camp to General Washington. Among four other historical paintings is John Chapman's portrayal of the baptism at Jamestown of Pocahontas, the Indian teenager who made a transition from a stone age culture to the British Court and kept peace between English colonists and Indians.

Of interest too is Gutzon Borglum's powerful carving in marble of Lincoln's head. "You will find written on his face literally all the complexity of his great nature... half smile, half sadness; half anger, half forgiveness... a dual nature struggling with a dual problem, delivering a single result," said Borglum.

Also gracing the Rotunda is a bronze reproduction of Houdon's life-sized marble statue of George Washington, done from life. The marble stands in the Rotunda of Virginia's Capitol in Richmond. The National Gallery of Art sought to borrow the original for an exhibition during the Bicentennial years. The hospitable state Washington loved surely would lend his likeness to the city he planned.

In the old Senate Chamber, responding to the challenge of states rights, Daniel Webster reached the summit of his eloquence, booming: "Liberty and Union, now and forever, one and inseparable!" Later, casting a vote for preserving the Union through the Missouri Compromise, he cast away his own chances of becoming President. The persistent fascination of Senate and House of Representatives is that the challenges and responses keep recurring.

With six-year terms, the 100 Senators tend to be lordly lions, at least between election years. With two-year terms the 435 House members are busy beavers, mending dams, slapping the water with alarm.

Occasionally a House members goes to greater things. When newly sworn-in President Gerald Ford addressed in 1974 a Joint Session he began by observing how good it was to be back in the "people's House." And sometimes a great one comes back, as did former President John Quincy Adams, winning a seat in the Twenty-second Congress. "My election as President... was not half so gratifying to my inmost soul," he confided in 1830 to his diary. And in the House he broke, after a long struggle, a Southern ban on debate over slavery.

At any rate the House beavers have the satisfaction of working in the largest, handsomest legislative pond in the world.

The Capitol houses more than 500 works of art. The greatest concentration of sculpture is in Statuary Hall, which served as the House wing between 1807 and 1857. Henry Clay presided there for two periods totaling 21 years and helped force passage of the Missouri compromise in 1819. In the course of the debate, Virginia's John Randolph pointed to the gallery and exclaimed: "Mr. Speaker, what, pray, are all these women doing here, so out of place in this arena? Sir, they had much better be at home attending to their knitting!"

When the Representatives moved to new quarters, the vast chamber became a marketplace filled with "cobwebs, apple cores, and hucksters' carts." In debating in 1864 whether to transform it into a "national Valhalla," one member declared: "I look to see where Clay sat, and I find a woman selling oranges and root beer!"

What the visitor sees today is scarcely less astonishing. Each state had a free hand choosing two distinguished citizens. Only a young, growing democracy could have invoked such an assemblage of bronze and marble figures, so varied in artistic worth and subject, as lines the walls.

In one fortuitous, dynamic grouping are statues of Senator Robert M. La Follette Sr. of Wisconsin, done compellingly in marble by Jo Davidson, rising massively from his chair to speak for the workingman; Louisiana's Huey Long, baleful in bronze, but combed and slicked up as if for Sunday School, not the pudgy, tousled Kingfish, who amused the Senate with a filibuster stuffed with Biblical quotations and the virtues of pot likker and, promising "Every Man a King," touched a deep chord during the Depression and frightened Franklin Roosevelt; and William Jennings Bryan, boy orator, of Nebraska, thrice a losing candidate for President, able Secretary of State for Woodrow Wilson, and defender of orthodoxy in Tennessee's Scopes trial. As its other son, Nebraska picked J. Sterling Morton, "Father of Arbor Day," reminder of a time when a community did its duty to the environment by planting a tree once a year.

Good, bad, or indifferent, the selections offer insights into the states. William Henry Harrison Beadle's name may not ring bells in eastern minds but a generation ago South Dakota's youth knew

Suffragettes, Congresswomen won't give up

Determined suffragettes, above, Elizabeth Cady Stanton, Susan B. Anthony, Lucretia Mott, stand fast in Capitol crypt; below, Congresswomen Martha Griffiths, Margaret Heckler, and Edith Green continue the good fight for women's rights.

Fine art brightens walls of
Capitol's huge Rotunda.
Bronze replica of Houdon's
famous marble statue of
George Washington stands
at left. In the center is
John Turnbull's painting of
Thomas Jefferson, in
red waistcoat, presenting
the Declaration of
Independence to Congress.
Turnbull served as
George Washington's aide,
and painted several of the
Founders from life. At
right is Gutzon Borg-
lum's massive carving of the
head of Abraham Lincoln.

Rotunda offers seat to rest and view art

In the center of the Capitol is the Rotunda

Directly under the dome and measuring 97 feet across, the Rotunda is the main intersection and a vast museum. Encircling its walls are statues of statesmen and eight huge paintings of major historical events. The marble statues, left to right, are Alexander Hamilton, Abraham Lincoln, Borglum's head of Lincoln, and President James Garfield.

Tulips stage a dazzling parade along the Capitol's East Front. Senate side is to the right, House side is to the left, a

e Rotunda crowns the center. On stands built on the Rotunda steps, the President is inaugurated every four years.

Night and Day the Capitol is a beacon

On a summer evening, left, the broad plaza before the Capitol's East Front becomes an ample stage for a band concert. The spacious flight of steps to the East Portico serves admirably to seat the audience. The setting is unique. No matter how grand or martial the music, it will be in proportion with the surroundings. By day, the Washingtonian only has to look up to the white dome to figure where he is.

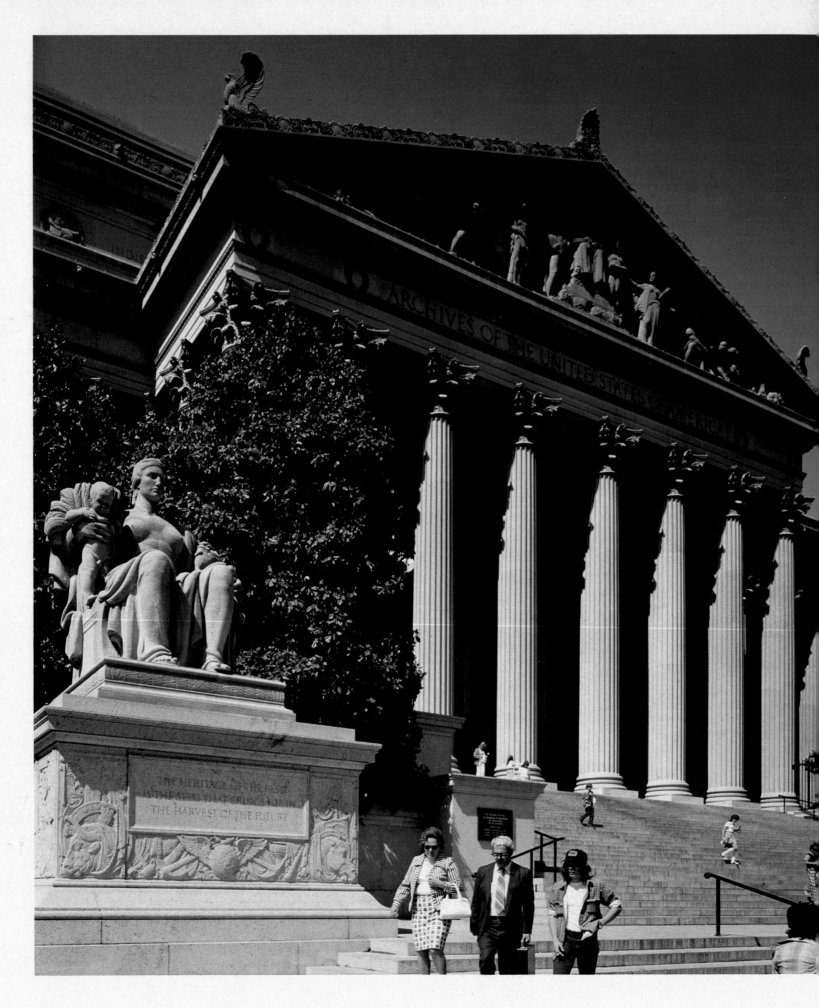

Readers use Library of Congress

National Archives, left, houses country's charters: Declaration of Independence, Constitution, and Bill of Rights. In the Library of Congress, right, readers peruse books at desks in the Main Reading Room. Interior of golden dome rises 160 feet. Never were more splendid surroundings in which to read and ruminate.

Visitors study the nations great charters

On an altar-like platform in the Exhibition Hall of the National Archives is a display of the three great documents forming the foundation of the United States: the Declaration of Independence, the Constitution, and the Bill of Rights. Murals by Barry Faulkner depict two great moments. Thomas Jefferson and his committee, left, present the Declaration to John Hancock, president of the Continental Congress. James Madison, right, submits the Constitution to George Washington and the Constitutional Convention. Behind the Exhibition Hall a circular gallery displays more than 250 items telling the histories of each of the 50 states.

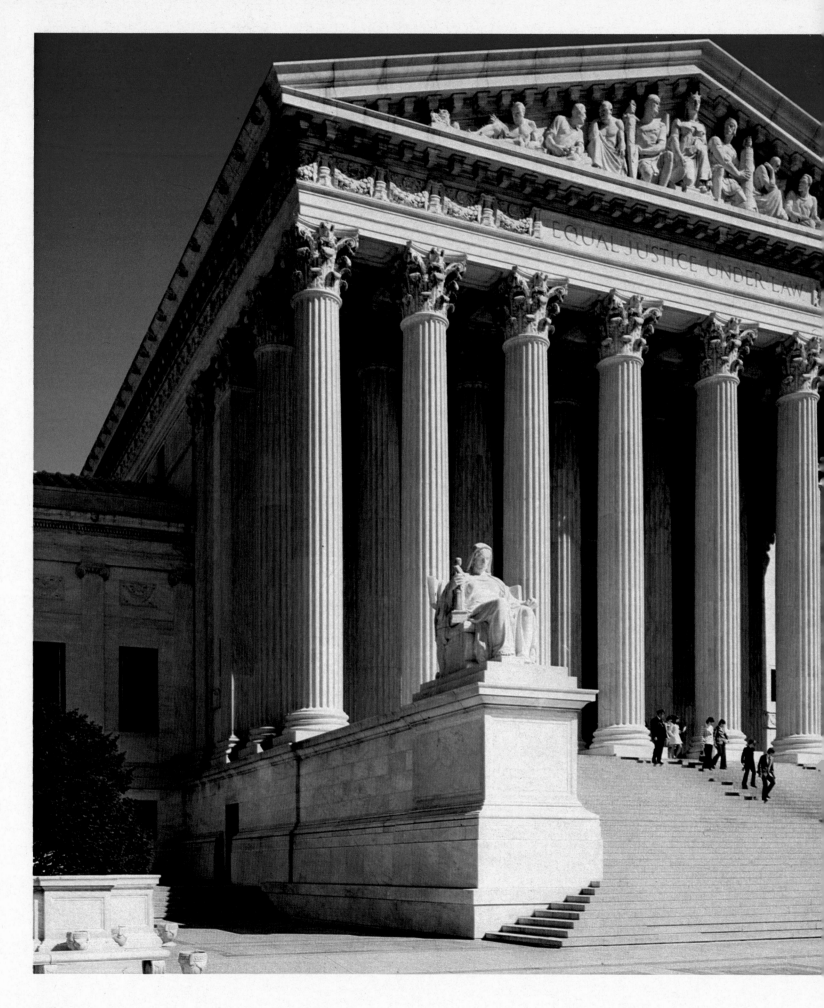

108

Supreme Court sits in temple of justice

Over the Supreme Court's portico are engraven four words – Equal Justice Under Law – the principle that guides the Chief Justice and eight Associate Justices in deliberating on cases and delivering opinions affecting every aspect of life in the United States.

Franklin keeps an eye on Penn's Avenue

One of Washington's most attractive statues, to pigeons, anyway, is that one honoring Benjamin Franklin on Pennsylvania Avenue at 10th Street. Pigeons flutter around him like so many aphorisms. Behind him is the frowning front of the Federal Bureau of Investigation.

Standing in front of the U.S. Treasury building is a statue honoring Alexander Hamilton, the first Secretary of the Treasury, who put the Nation's fiscal structure on a sound footing. Looking down on Hamilton is a Union sentry standing at one corner of a monument honoring General William T. Sherman. The Treasury Building is the oldest of the departmental structures and makes a fine photographers stand for parades coming up Pennsylvania Avenue. Architect Robert Mills designed it handsomely.

he saved 20 million acres of school lands in the West. Georgia's pupils heard through six grades about Dr. Crawford W. Long and wished mightily he had discovered something easier to spell than anesthesia.

Southern states tend to look back by slipping a favorite Confederate into the arena and then look forward by introducing an educator. Alabama presents "Fightin'" Joe Wheeler, rebel, and J. L. M. Curry, an apostle of education as an agent for philanthropies for white and black schools. North Carolina bowed to Civil War Governor Zebulon B. Vance and then saluted a turn-of-the-century Governor, Charles B. Aycock. At the unveiling in 1932 the National Education Association said that Aycock "did for education in North Carolina what Horace Mann did for it in Massachusetts." Texas chose Sam Houston, who led it into statehood and then resigned as Governor rather than sign the oath of allegiance to the Confederacy. Roger Williams is represented carrying a Bible. Welcomed to the Massachusetts Colony as "a godly minister," banished five years later in 1635 for "dangerous opinions," he planted Rhode Island on the notion that a person's beliefs were a matter of his own conscience.

In the corridor leading from Statuary Hall to the House is Jo Davidson's statue of Will Rogers slouched, hands shoved in pockets, head bent, the beginnings of a grin on his face, ready to look up and drawl that when Congressmen "get in that immense hall, they begin to get serious, and it's then they do such amusing things."

A plaque in the floor of Statuary Hall marks the spot where John Quincy Adams collapsed at 81 from a stroke on February 21, 1848. Two days later he died on a couch in the Speaker's Office just off the chamber.

Standing where Adams stood, a person can hear a whisper across the room. The acoustical curiosity is a popular stop on guided tours of the Capitol. The guide stations his group properly, then walks across the room, bends down, and whispers, "All those who can hear me, raise your hands." And they do.

Overflowing Statuary Hall, the figures have been placed along the Hall of Columns or in corridors around the building. Mark Twain called the Capitol's collection a "delirium tremens" of art. But some pieces are choice and nearly all are edifying, one way or another. To walk the corridors and see the figures of the past in striking poses and occasionally glimpse a celebrated Senator stalking the hall or a famous House member hurrying by conveys at times a startling sense of intermingling of tenses.

The most derided statue is in the Crypt, a circular hall directly under the Rotunda. With massive, squat columns supporting a groined arched ceiling, the Crypt seems a thick-set forest

White House glistens amid greenery

The White House, the nation's Executive Mansion, rests resplendent on a knoll among trees, fountains, and green lawns. To its right is the old State, War, Navy building, "anchor to the city," which also houses some Executive offices.

of toadstools, the columns forming the stalks and the arches the sheltering caps. To one side is Adelaide Johnson's sculptural study of three early suffragettes – Lucretia Mott, Susan B. Anthony, and Elizabeth Cady Stanton – commonly known as "Three Suffragettes in a Tub." Whether or not it is good art, it is memorable and pertinent. They were comrades in good causes throughout the last half of the 19th century, just as they appear to be, emerging shoulder to shoulder from the 8-ton marble block, an indomitable trio.

Mrs. Stanton and Miss Anthony helped publish *The Revolution*, a defiant periodical. "We said at all times just what we thought," said Mrs. Stanton, "and advertised nothing we did not believe in." Mrs. Stanton and Mrs. Mott found time, amid crusades, to make pleasant homes for their broods of children. Iron-willed Susan was not forbidding in appearance. For a time she wore the blouse and Turkish trousers advocated by Amelia Bloomer but abandoned it after a year. "I found it a physical comfort, but a mental crucifixtion," she said. One reform at a time, she decided.

Lips firmly compressed, determined to represent women, blacks, and other minorities who had endured so much so long in silence, the sculptured triad is a moving sight.

To pay respects to them came three members of the House. Democrats Edith Green of Oregon and Martha Griffiths of Michigan and Republican, Margaret Heckler of Massachusetts. Mrs. Green looked, deceptively, as if she would be more at ease pulling biscuits out of the oven than bills out of the fire; Mrs. Griffiths, wise-eyed, determined, and Mrs. Heckler, redheaded, quickminded.

The Equal Rights Amendment had been introduced regularly since 1923 without success. The Judiciary Committee had not held a hearing on it in a generation.

"There were no women on the committee," explained Mrs. Griffiths.

In 1972 she forced ERA out of committee.

"Tell how you did it, Martha," said Mrs. Green.

"I stood in the well of the floor," said Mrs. Griffiths, "and as I saw each of the 13 chairmen, I asked him please to sign the discharge petition, and took him by the hand, and he did."

Mrs. Green succeeded after nine years in guiding to passage in 1962 her equal-pay-for-equal-work bill.

"Earlier," she said, "when the Chairman of the Labor Subcommittee handled the equal-pay bill, he filed it, facetiously, under B for broads."

In 1959–60, managing John F. Kennedy's Presidential campaign in Oregon, she recruited his backing for her bill.

"When we were riding around Oregon, we discussed it," said Mrs. Green, "and then as President he supported it."

Lafayette
and chess players
occupy Square

114

Lafayette Square is Washington's town square. In early years when handsome residences surrounded the Square, it was called the "lobby" to the White House across Pennsylvania Avenue. On the southwest corner of the Square is a heroic bronze statue honoring General Lafayette.

Four other French heroes, stationed at the base of the statue, pay Lafayette homage. They are Comte d'Estaing and Comte de Grasse offering naval aid and Comte de Rochambeau and Chevalier Duportail extending military help. Blair House, upper right, is the nation's Guest House.

Andrew Jackson doffs his hat to White House

In Lafayette Square a girl poses for a snapshot. In the background, at 1600 Pennsylvania Avenue, is the North Portico of the White House. From stands at this point along the Avenue, each President views the parade that follows his Inauguration at the Capitol. Andrew Jackson's statue occupies the center of the Square. The first equestrian figure in the United States, it was cast from bronze cannon captured by Jackson in the War of 1812. Clark Mills, the artist, designed the figure so that the center of balance is at the horse's hind feet.

116

Mrs. Heckler, advocate of the Child and Family Services Act, also persuaded the Republican National Convention to endorse a platform plank for care centers for children of working women.

How did the House treat the 16 women?

"The seniority system has been the big protection for women and other minorities," observed Mrs. Green. "In Congress they can't bar you from moving up the committees' ladders to chairmanships."

"All you have to do is continue to get elected," said Mrs. Griffiths.

That, Mrs. Heckler observed, was the difference between the political parties and Congress.

"The parties have not come to grips with the issue of equality," she said.

What reason did male congressmen advance for resisting bills for women's rights?

"Vive le difference!" the women chorused — and smiled at male pretense in denying fair play under guise of gallantry.

"I feel I must work for a broad spectrum," said one. "I feel I represent my district and all women of America!"

Who said it? No way of knowing. They were leaving the toadstool forest, chatting and laughing, shoulder to shoulder.

Stretching below the West Front 252 feet along First Street at the Capitol end of the Mall is the Grant Memorial designed by Henry Merwin Shrady.

On a towering central pedestal sits General Ulysses Grant, the second largest such bronze in the world. Below Grant at each end of the long granite base Union cavalrymen are in action.

It was a hot day. Still. Nothing stirred. On the broad face of the Capitol's West Front, the Flag drooped, a melting peppermint stick.

Below the Capitol, on curving First Street, like a red, white, and blue furbelow, were parked bright-colored trucks, with sides that opened into stalls, waiting for tourists to buy ice cream.

Among the hucksters was an ice cream salesman his red face seemed a sweaty duplicate of the sun.

"Nice hot day," he said. He looked around. Nobody was buying.

"But no people," he added. "Too much crime."

It was 2 in the afternoon, so sultry the Washington Monument loomed through the haze is if only a block away. The Monument looked so pale, it might faint. A white wax candle.

Before the salesman lay the reflecting pool, idly reflecting.

"Lyndon Johnson did that," said the salesman.

A sign — Capitol Reflecting Pool — supplied statistics: started April 29, 1968; completed May 24, 1972; capacity, 2,500,000 gallons . . .

"He put that there," said the ice cream man.

He made it seem that LBJ had come over personally from the White House, dug it, and hosed in the water, all for Lady Bird.

High above the scene on a bronze horse was. Grant, hunched in a military greatcoat, an old slouch hat pulled low over his eyes.

The north end of the Memorial is especially picturesque, a frenzied cavalry charge welded by momentum into one rushing mass. The commander, mouth squared in a shout, eyes bulged, holds aloft a broken sword.

Under foot is a fallen horse and rider, the horse resigned, the man bemused, cloak thrown over his head like a security blanket, content in his sudden removal from the thunder overhead.

Above it all, Grant, slumping, looks bone tired.

"I can't spare this man," Lincoln told critics. "He fights."

Suddenly the cavalry charge was animated by a father and five boys investigating the action. The mother stood watching.

"This could be stumps sticking up," said the oldest boy, pointing to the rough surface under the horses' hoofs.

"Horses could never go on rocks like that," said the father. The boys were clambering all around the statur.

"It must be water. I can't see their hoofs," said one.

"That's it," said the father. "This leading horse is on solid ground with his front feet. They're fording a stream."

He was, he said, a Pennsylvania ironworker.

"C'mon," he called, "Let's get some ice cream." They retreated. Grant sat motionless.

Lobbyists in the Capitol fall into three categories; business and industrial spokesmen, local and state officials, and issue-oriented individuals.

In a Capitol restaurant eating a salad was a ruddy-faced lobbyist. His job was to circulate a monthly letter among manufacturers about bills affecting their product's sale. He relished being in Washington, hearing on the car radio weather reports for Rome, London, and Paris, observing in televised news how events abroad registered on Washington's seismograph, and knowing, although he had never visited it, that the Kennedy Center was there. His time was absorbed in getting out the news letter and looking after his yard in the Virginia suburbs. Crab grass was his Cyprus.

"I'll never go back to Cleveland," he said.

On a Saturday feeding the ducks by a pond in the National Arboretum were issue-oriented Diane and Michael Jones, Diane's arm, when she reached out her hand to feed a black swan, arched as gracefully as the swan's neck. Michael, serious-eyed, mild-mannered, straight-spoken, said they had taken off the morning from work with the five-member staff of the Coalition to Stop Funding the War. Their office on Maryland Avenue was within sight of the Capitol.

Graduates of Reed College in Portland, Diane in Math and Michael in philosophy, they worked with the Peace Corps in Malaysia two years and with the American Friends Service Committee in Saigon for two and a half years.

They seemed, that morning in the park, crusaders.

"I don't think we're necessarily crusaders," said Diane.

"We want to do what we can to change American policy in a part of the world we know something about," said Michael. "We learned to speak the Vietnamese language and came to think very Highly of the Vietnamese people and were upset that our country's government had come half way around the world to that country to fight a war, for reasons which I think are still really difficult to ascertain."

Wasn't it over now?

"When we went back in February of 1974 for four months to fill a personnel gap for the Friends, we found American money and guns still feeding a war-based government that keeps the war going," said Michael. "That's why we think Congress has a good opportunity to end American involvement simply by controlling the purse."

They planned to re-enter school, Diane to become a lawyer and Michael to learn graphics that might be useful in socially oriented projects.

What aroused their concern for society?

"We grew up in the 1960s, like everybody else our age, and that probably had a lot to do with it," said Michael. "Many basic contradictions in American society and a lot of the negative aspects of the American way of life and foreign policy became observable through the Vietnamese War.

"We try to learn what Congress is considering about Indochina and mail the information to interested organizations and individuals to let them know what amendments we think people should support or oppose."

Diane fed the last bite of bread to the last duck, and they pedaled back to the Vietnamese War.

Under the National Archives broad portico, Morris Ball raised his hand and called to 50 chattering junior high school students from Union, New Jersey: "Now, whoever has the buzzer, put it away. The boy who had one of those last year never got it back."

"Now remember, inside you'll see our country's birth certificates. The original documents of the Declaration of Independence and the Constitution and Bill of Rights. When these papers were brought here, they were turning yellow and disintegrating. Now they are exhibited in cases filled with helium to stop the deterioration. At night, or in an emergency, an elevator lowers them into a vault.

"Let's go in here quietly," he said, and the class began to troop through the huge doors.

He had been teaching, he told a bystander, 21 years. Only the other week a former student, a lawyer, had mentioned that he still had his scrapbook on The Living Constitution.

"I have the students clip articles that show how the daily news relates to the Constitution and cite the sections. A scrapbook of 50 articles gets the top mark."

What basic point did he make about the birth certificates?

"That we have a government of laws that provides safety for all. There's no dictator here. We've lasted this long and come through many troubles. There must be something good about our government. I'm willing to bring students down here every year because it's important they see the good things."

The good things they saw were the Declaration of Independence, a single sheet of parchment encased between green marble columns. Spread below it in a panel are pages one and four of the Constitution's five pages and the Bill of Rights.

In the Continental Congress meeting in Philadelphia a committee of five was appointed on June 11, 1776 to prepare the Declaration. Jefferson was chairman. The others were John Adams, Benjamin Franklin, Roger Sherman, and Robert R. Livingston.

At his portable writing desk in his Philadelphia boardinghouse, Jefferson penned the announcement of the birth of a nation: "We hold these truths to be self-evident: that all men are created equal; that they are endowed by their Creator with inherent and inalienable rights; that among these are life, liberty, and the pursuit of happiness..."

Jefferson first submitted it to Adams and Franklin for corrections and then to the Congress, He remembered with deep gratitude that Adams "supported the Declaration with zeal and ability, fighting fearlessly for every word of it." Adams was, said Jefferson, "the pillar of its support on the floor of Congress, its ablest advocate and defender against the multifarious assaults it encountered." Another member called Adams "the Atlas of American independence."

What grieved the two friends most was the action of Congress in deleting Jefferson's denunciation of Britain's slave trade, a "cruel war against human nature itself." Looking back, Jefferson said that the clause was stricken "in complaisance to South Carolina and Georgia, who had never attempted to restrain the importation of slaves, and who, on the contrary, still wished to continue it. Our Northern brethren also, I believe, felt a little tender under those censures; for though their people had very few slaves themselves, yet they had been pretty considerable carriers of them to others."

The politics of their parties parted Jefferson and Adams, but late in life they renewed their deep friendship and a rich correspondence.

Jefferson enjoyed the New Englander's tartness and Adams prized the Virginian's sunniness. Writ-

ing from Monticello to Adams on August 1, 1816, Jefferson said: "My temperament is sanguine. I steer my bark with Hope in the head, leaving Fears astern. My hopes, indeed, sometimes fail; but not oftener than the forebodings of the gloomy."

Would Jefferson agree to live his 73 years over again forever, Adams asked.

"I hesitate to say," responded Jefferson, "From twenty-five to sixty, I would say yes; and I might go further back, but not come lower down... There is a ripeness of time for death, regarding others as well as ourselves, when it is reasonable we should drop off and make room for other growth. When we have lived our generation out, we should not wish to encroach on another. I enjoy good health; I am happy in what is around me, yet I assure you I am ripe for leaving all, this year, this day, this hour."

Both Adams and Jefferson died July 4, 1826, the 50th anniversary of the Declaration.

On the evening of July 3 Jefferson roused himself, and, in his last words, asked: "Is it the Fourth?"

He died at one o'clock on the afternoon of the Fourth. In the dawn of the Fourth in Massachusetts, Adams awoke.

"Do you know, sir, what day this is?" a servant asked.

"O yes," said Adams, "it is the glorious Fourth of July. God bless it. God bless you all!"

In the afternoon, he revived again, and, not knowing Jefferson had preceded him a little time, he said, in his last words: "Thomas Jefferson survives."

In the Archives building's foyer is a working model of the mechanism that lowers the documents into the vault. The display is nearly as popular with some persons, the guides note, as are the original documents.

The vital test, as Morris Ball puts it to his students, is whether the great creeds are working in the minds of Americans.

In the Library of Congress just east of the Capitol, a reader knows he has come into his own. There are 270 miles of shelves and 85 million items. But more telling than those statistics is a sign on a stand outside the main reading room: "READERS ONLY. Visitors may view the reading room from the visitors gallery."

When the original library was destroyed by the British in 1814, Thomas Jefferson offered as a replacement, at whatever value Congress cared to put on it, his own library collected over 50 years. "I do not know," he wrote, "that it contains any branch of science which Congress would wish to exclude from their collection; there is, in fact, no subject to which a Member of Congress may not have occasion to refer."

Nothing in the Library matches the sight of the marble-pillared Main Reading Room, rising

160 feet. In a concentric circle are the 200 curved desks for readers. The shining interior is like a great golden hive, stacked with combs.

A mile and a half from the Capitol at 1600 Pennsylvania Avenue is the White House, the Executive Mansion which Charles Dickens termed an "English clubhouse" and Jefferson "big enough for two emperors, one Pope, and the Grand Lama." In 1792 the design earned James Hoban, an Irish architect practicing in Charleston, South Carolina, a gold medal worth $500.

To Americans it seems just right, and, with all the expansions for the sake of effectiveness, remains graceful and unpretentious. There is a frequent turnover of occupants, each of whom nevertheless leaves some loving touches. Jackson left a great coffee cup; Mrs. Coolidge, a crocheted bedspread, on which she had worked two years, for the Lincoln nine-foot four-poster bed; the Trumans, a balcony on the second floor level of the South Portico.

Something of the immensity of the President's responsibility was conveyed by Eleanor Roosevelt when, after learning of her husband's death, she informed Vice President Truman. Feeling, he said later, as if the universe had fallen on him like a load of hay, Truman asked what he could do for her.

"Is there anything *we* can do for *you*?" she replied. "For you are the one in trouble now."

Often called FDR's eyes and ears, Mrs. Roosevelt served as well as a guide for the nation, taking Americans by the hand into coal mines, slums, and wherever else her heart led her.

Part of the excitement of being in Washington is the sight of a Congressmen getting in a taxicab or even a President in passing.

Near the White House in the Blue Dawn Restaurant, Mrs. Aleen Green, an employe there for 13 years, remarked: "It's as good as any other city. I'll put it this way: you meet interesting people when you least expect it.

"I waited on President Kennedy. It was in August, 1962, about 3 o'clock in the afternoon. I recognized him and said, 'Hi!' and shook his hand."

What did he order?

"Fried shrimp."

And what did they talk about?

"Children. We talked about his little boy, who had just had his picture in the paper, playing under the President's desk. He was laughing and saying he didn't know at first the boy was under there. That tickled him."

John Adams, the first resident of the White House, had a prayer for all the others, which Franklin Roosevelt had carved on the mantel in the State Dining Room:

"I Pray Heaven to Bestow the Best of Blessings on THIS HOUSE and on All that shall hereafter Inhabit it. May none but Honest and Wise Men ever rule under this Roof."

Executive offices overlook green park

Tulips put out colors and First Division Memorial rises before the old State, War, Navy Building, now housing Executive offices. Marble shaft 88 feet high and bronze Victory commemorate Division's dead lantly during World War I.

Sen. Mike Mansfield leads the Majority

Congress was adjourning for a recess, and tall, spare Senate Majority Leader Mike Mansfield, striding into his office suite, tossed an "Okay!" to his visitors and led them into the inner office.

"Well, shoot!" said Mansfield.

What characteristic was most important to a Majority Leader?

"It depends on the Majority Leader. I think patience is a requisite, understanding of the Senate and its procedures, cooperation with the Minority Leader, and a recognition that all Senators are equal. There are no superior or inferior Senators and regardless of their length of service or the prestige which they achieve, it is a body of peers."

Senator Mansfield has a face as bleak, with a kind of closed watchfulness, as one of his Montana cliffsides. Yet because it normally is expressionless as a slate, the least emotion enlivens it like a shaft of sunlight striking the mountain, and observers rejoice at the phenomenon. No one thinks of him as Michael Joseph, but Mike. Mike Mansfield, Democrat of Montana — it all runs together like a formidable range.

In 1961 there had been speculation that the Senator was "too nice" to be Majority Leader.

"Yes, that charge has been made," said the Senator. "Although I look upon it as a compliment, really. Because I don't believe in cracking the whip or twisting arms, making demands. I hope through logic and persuasion and reasonableness that I can get enough of my colleagues to see my point of view." There was a long pause, and he added, "And besides, I would like to be treated by my colleagues as I treat them; and I would stack the record of my almost 14 years as Majority Leader against the record of any previous Majority Leader, because I think the record has to speak for itself, and that's all that counts."

He talks, barely opening his lips, as if speech was something precious, to be husbanded. Reflective silences stretch away between Mansfield's comments, so that phrases are left to stand as sentences, buttes on an arid landscape. Yet they parse, and a vein of eloquence runs through them.

What in his background equipped him to work as Majority Leader?

"Probably the fact that I rarely become too opinionated, and I recognize that there are two sides and sometimes more to every question. And maybe the other fellow is right and I'm wrong."

Son of Irish immigrants — his father worked as a porter in a New York City hotel — he was taken at 3, when his mother died, to live with relatives in Great Falls, Montana. At 14 he fibbed about his age and enlisted in the World War I Navy, then in the Army for a year, and the Marines for two years and served in the Philippines and China. "I wanted to see the world. I wanted to help my country, and I imagine it was there that I learned discipline and to control myself, and maybe it stuck with me through the years."

Had he worked hard as a child?

"Not too hard. Hard enough. The only jobs I had were pushing a grocery cart, working on ranches in the summer, and as a whistle punk signaling the donkey engine hauling logs in the woods. After the Navy, I worked nine years in the mines as a mucker, or shoveler, and an assistant mining engineer, and after that I was a student, a professor, and a member of Congress."

What prompted him to resume his education?

"Oh, I met a girl in Butte. Her name was Maureen Hayes. She was teaching in the Butte High School. We began going together. I told her I hadn't finished the eighth grade. She thought I ought to get an education, and, of course, I noticed the men in the mines didn't live to ripe old ages." Making up high school credits as he went along, he studied a year at the Montana School of Mines and then in 1930 entered Montana State University. "The Butte high school teacher came down in '31 and we were married. She cashed her insurance and put me through school, and I got a B. A. degree in '33, stayed another year for my M. A., and went on the faculty as an instructor."

How did he become interested in public office?

"Again my wife. She thought there was an opening, and that I should make the effort, and I did. Course, she's paid a pretty high price since that time in loneliness and a lack of a good family life."

Were there other influential figures?

"There were three. One was Senator Thomas Walsh of Montana, who in my opinion was one of the great Senators of the Republic. I only saw him twice, but I always admired him and his chairmanship of the Teapot Dome Investigation.

"Another was Charlie Russell, an old cowboy artist to whom I used to deliver groceries in Great Falls. I became interested in his paintings and sketches and letters in the Mint Saloon downtown where I used to sell julep leaves and empty bottles to the bartender. He used to give away his sketches for drinks, but when he married Alice Cooper, she developed his talent for the sale of his pictures. He was a blood brother to the Blackfeet, and he understood the Indians, and the immigrants and the settlers and cowboys and ranch owners, and the people in small towns. I just liked his wit, his style, his painting and his honesty.

"The third was John F. Kennedy. We had served together in the House and Senate and become quite friendly. I didn't want to be Majority Leader, but he and Dick Russell and Johnson and three or four others asked me, and finally I did. We didn't

"There are no superior or inferior Senators and regardless of their length of service or prestige which they achieve, it is a body of peers," says Mike Mansfield.

123

always agree, but we always understood each other, and I felt that he was just on the verge of becoming an excellent President, maybe a great one. But time cut him short, and... that was it."

Why didn't he want to be Majority Leader?

"Because I was happy and satisfied just being a Senator from the State of Montana, which was far more than I had ever hoped for, and just felt that I had gone as far as I wanted to go."

Did he have doubts about his capacity?

"Oh, yes. I've had doubts about my capacity as professor, before I came here, as a Congressman and as a Senator, as a Majority Leader – and I still have those doubts."

Was it incongruous for a Senator of the Far West to be interested in the Far East?

"Remember I was in the service and traveled. Then, while spending a year or so in China, I developed an interest in the Far East and kept it alive through reading even while in the mines. My major work for my degrees was in Far Eastern history, and when I came here I was placed on the Foreign Affairs Committee in the House and then on the Foreign Relations Committee in the Senate."

Of what was he proudest in his record as Majority Leader?

"My excellent relationship with Republican Leaders Dirksen and Scott, and my relationship to the Senate as a whole."

Did any of his bills give him particular satisfaction?

"Yes. Getting the vote for the 18-years-olds through statutory legislation and having that upheld by the Supreme Court. The reason for it was to give the youngsters a piece of the action rather than keep them out on the sidelines, to find a way to get them to participate directly in politics. Also to bring about a better recognition of their responsibilities. At 18 if they came into conflict with the law, they were tried in adult courts. At

18 they could sign contracts and be liable, could marry, were liable for the draft. So, I wanted to see it rounded out, and as long as they had to assume those responsibilities, give them something to make them direct participants in politics and in the making of the laws, indirect though it might be, to which they were subject."

Had he any fears about the system's surviving Watergate?

"None at all! None at all! Because while we are going through a purgatory of sorts now, I think that out of it will come a stronger nation, a better informed people, and a more direct participation by the people in scrutinizing their elected officials and candidates for office. There will also be a closer scrutinizing of campaign finances. We'll be held to a far greater accountability. I have no doubt that the Republic will survive and be the better for it after we pass through these troubled times."

Had Washington changed much during his career?

"You have all these concrete and glass buildings, and the atmosphere has been taken away. It's really a big city now. When I came, it was sort of a middle-sized city, with a lot of old dwellings and a slower pace."

What has been the greatest change in the Nation since he came to Washington in 1942?

"Oh, it's become too urbanized, and partly as a result, there's been a tremendous increase in crime. The small city has decayed. The small ranches are being replaced by corporate outfits. We've become more materialistic-minded and more interested in ourselves than in our fellows."

What does the United States need most?

"Straightforwardness. Even when you make mistakes, and I think people'll understand. I'm not pessimistic. I'm saddened by what's happening. But I'm not pessimistic because I just can't afford to be." The Majority Leader's chin went up, and he said: "I won't be."

John Brademas looks for expertise

Representative John Brademas, looking over a foot-deep drift of papers that nearly buried his desk, remarked seriously that what Congress needs is Operative Access to Relevant Intelligence.

"One of my preoccupations," said the Democrats' Chief Deputy Whip, "is how Congress can get expertise on which the Executive Branch has had a monopoly. It's got to be operative – you must be able to get at it, or it doesn't do you much good. You want access. You don't want everything; you only want what's relevant. And you want more than information. Information can come pouring in on you. You want intelligence."

There's a need, he said, to develop more effective linkages between House members and authorities on the matters with which Congress deals.

"As Chairman of the Education Subcommittee, how do I get access to the best thinking in the country in that field? We are not easily geared up to tap those sources.

"We've moved ahead by establishing our own budgetary office here on Capitol Hill. Up until now the Executive branch has had an monopoly of expertise."

He paused and smiled. "I'm reminded of what President Johnson once remarked. 'My problem,' he said, 'is not so much *doing* what is right as *knowing* what is right.'"

To the observation that his own overloaded desk appeared to bear out the need, the Indiana Democrat laughed. His staff, he said, once posted a picture of the desk captioned with a quote he frequently cites from Spinoza: "Order is in the mind."

Isn't it rare to find a Hoosier politician, or any for that matter, spouting Spinoza?

Not in a state where everybody is a potential candidate for office, said Brademas, adding: "Charlie Halleck, a friend and the former Minority Leader of the House, used to say that the

first words uttered by every baby born in Indiana are: 'I am not a candidate but if nominated and elected I will serve!'"

A confluence of factors, he said, propelled him into politics: his mother, an Indiana school teacher; his father, a Greek immigrant, who instilled in him the idea that the Greeks invented Democracy, and his grandfather, a high school superintendent, with whom the boy spent the summers.

"If grandfather thought politics was important, why it must be", he said. "Then the Methodist Church, with its concern for social problems, had a considerable effect on my attitude."

In the Navy he spent a year at the University of Mississippi, went to Harvard four years for his B.A. degree and graduate work in international studies and then to Oxford as a Rhodes Scholar for a Ph.D in social studies.

At Oxford he considered going into the foreign service, but was "appalled at the failure of John Foster Dulles to defend career officers against attacks by Senator Joseph McCarthy. I didn't want to get in that position. I wanted to talk back. I came back and ran at 26 for Congress and lost with 49.5 per cent of the vote. I didn't earn enough money in 1954 to file a Federal income tax, but I almost got elected to Congress. I directed research for Adlai Stevenson's Presidential campaign through the Chicago convention of 1956, after which I ran for Congress again and lost in the Eisenhower landslide. So there I was, not yet 30, twice defeated for Congress, a has-been before I started. I taught political science in South

"One of my preoccupations is how Congress can get expertise on which the Executive branch has had a monopoly," says Chief Deputy Whip John Brademas.

Bend at St. Mary's College, ran in 1958, and won."

Education is his primary interest. He sponsored the bill that established the National Institute of Education to support research in teaching and, working with Rhode Island Senator Pell who proposed the idea, helped frame that basic opportunity grant for college-age youths. In Congress he admires House Speaker Carl Albert and Majority Leader Tip O'Neill and remembers with affection former House Speaker Sam Rayburn.

"My first year here we were struggling over the labor reform issue at a time when Jimmy Hoffa was a controversial figure. Four of us freshmen who had labor support nevertheless favored reform, and we were getting heat both ways. Speaker Rayburn called us in his office simply to say he was proud of what we were doing and would back us. Well, for freshmen to be offered support by the Speaker, a legendary figure in his own day, gave us a sense of nobility of mission in being part of the House of Representatives.

"I also admired Paul Douglas, my political godfather, who was chairman of the Democratic National Committee, a partisan but also a person with an intense commitment to justice. John Gardner's a good friend, although at the moment we're squabbling on a couple of matters."

Representative Brademas drew three lessons from Watergate: "First, we must not retreat from politics, the only instrument in a free society for making choices between ideas, candidates, and parties. Second, we must strengthen the role of Congress against the powers of the Presidency, and, third, we have to recover a sense of moral purpose in politics. The Nixon people got into trouble because they thought the purpose was to win and retain power by any means, but politics is the pursuit of justice and freedom for all people. That's what politics is all about."

Powers alarm Charles Mathias

Ruddy-faced, smoking a pipe, an olive-gold Chesapeake Bay retriever at his feet, Maryland Senator Charles McCurdy (Mac) Mathias Jr. looked like a country gentleman and scholar, with all the time in the world to philosophize. But he is strenuously engaged in shaping and pushing reforms as diverse as stopping the pollution of Chesapeake Bay and halting "the drift toward one-man government" in the United States. He was in the midst of a race for re-election in which he had pledged he would not accept any contribution that exceeded $100.

Born in Frederick, Md., educated in public schools and at Haverford College and the University of Maryland Law School, he served during World War II on an amphibious command ship and was among the first Americans to see Nagasaki and Hiroshima. "Perhaps I'm the only member of Congress who has seen what happened when an atomic bomb hit a city. I'll tell you it's something you don't forget," he said.

He won a seat in the House in 1960, and when his father grumbled that "I'd left him with the whole load of the law office, I reminded him that in the spring of 1929 he had taken me with him to the White House to say goodbye to Calvin Coolidge. Right there, I told him, I got Potomac fever, and he was responsible."

He pointed to a picture on the wall. "That's Theodore Roosevelt and that's my grandfather, taken during the Bull Moose campaign of 1912," he said. "Occasionally when some stalwart Republicans question a vote as being on the liberal side, the really old-timers will say, 'What can you expect? His grandfather was as Bull Moose.'"

He mentioned some members he had watched and respected, a bipartisan list: Mike Mansfield, Hugh Scott, Harry Byrd Sr., and William Fulbright in the Senate, and Charlie Halleck, Emanuel Celler, and Sam Rayburn in the House. "Once I commented to Sam Rayburn that I had half a million constituents who could reach the Capitol with a local phone call, and he said, 'God help you, son! God help you!'"

From childhood he has been fascinated by the Chesapeake Bay as an amenity as well as a source of livelihood for the region. Now he and his wife and two sons fish, crab, and swim in its waters. "The Bay is savable. I don't think it's past the threshold of redemption," Charles Mathias said.

"To give you an idea of the magnitude of the task of cleaning the Bay," he said, "when the District of Columbia began treating sewage in the 1930s, the city was using the Potomac as an open sewer for a metropolitan population of 650,000. Now, nearly 40 years later, we are discharging into the Potomac the equivalent of a population of 750,000.

"But the Bay's need of help and the population's willingness to provide it appear to be coming together," he said. "Even the independent watermen, who resisted any regulation for sanitation traps on boats, now realize that something must be done when during a summer weekend the Bay is floating the equivalent of the combined population of Frederick and Hagerstown."

Watergate does not disillusion him about the system, which has demonstrated, he said, "a self-purification process.

"If the newspapers and broadcast media hadn't carried accounts of Watergate, if the Congress hadn't launched the impeachment process, if the courts hadn't become involved in cases, unhappy and tragic as each of these individual elements was, then, in fact, Watergate would have been a tragedy. But the fact that all of these unhappy events occurred, painful though they were to us, proved that the system's checks and balances worked."

"Right now we are living in four states of emergency... Each proclamation has provided Presidents with extraordinary powers...," says Sen. Charles Mathias.

127

But in a major respect the system needs strengthening, he believes.

In the House he was among several members who introduced the first plan for peace in Vietnam. When that failed, he introduced a measure for repeal of the Gulf of Tonkin resolution and other Cold War resolutions and just that morning had been working as co-chairman of the Senate's Special Committee studying emergency powers of the President.

"Through history, you know, abuse of such power has meant the disintegration of the democratic process," he said. "In Rome, the transition from a republic to the empire resulted from the abuse of emergency power.

"Right now, we are living in four states of emergency, the first having been proclaimed by Franklin Roosevelt in 1933. Each proclamation has provided Presidents with some extraordinary powers to control almost every aspect of our lives. In this century our country has gone through four wars, a major depression, and a series of crises, the energy shortage being the most recent, which have stimulated the flow of power to the executive."

The bipartisan committee, which he chairs with Senator Frank Church of Idaho, intends to recommend to Congress which of 470 emergency powers should be repealed. Guidelines would provide that in declaring a national emergency, a President would specify which statutes are being invoked and the reason for his action. At any time within six months, Congress could affirm or withdraw the President's statutory powers and would have to approve further extensions of six months.

"This may very well be my most important contribution because I think it will go further than almost any single thing we can do to prevent abuse of power of a kind which history has shown to be peculiarly dangerous," said Senator Mathias.

John B. Anderson heads GOP huddle

The greatest problem facing Congress in the mid-1970s?

"Finances," said Representative John B. Anderson. "Closer control of the budget."

The answers habitually come swiftly, with certitude, so much so that newsmen, catching him on the wing, are sometimes left groping for the next question while he is saying goodbye.

"The first step is to reduce spending and get the budget into balance. We've got to make some Draconian choices and establish national priorities in such a way that we spend less and spend it for those things that ought to be getting attention and defer some of the other nice things that might be good to have but, like I often tell my wife, we can't afford this year. Inflation is the number one problem; and government spending, for which Congress bears responsibility, certainly comes under that head."

The impression that the Illinois Republican is highly motivated, tightly scheduled, and closely organized seems confirmed in a background that includes a Phi Beta Kappa key from the University of Illinois, a Master of Law degree from Harvard, four battle stars from combat in France and Germany during World War II, selection in 1964 by the National Association of Evangelicals as Outstanding Layman of the Year, and election by his colleagues in 1969 as Chairman of the House Republican Conference.

He tends to be moderate – in 1967 he cast the vote in the Rules Committee which permitted the House to vote on open housing legislation – with a conservative bent on finances.

"I come from very, very modest means." he said, "and I was brought up with the work ethic thoroughly ingrained in my system. My spare time was not spent playing games but working in my father's grocery store. I suppose that has something to do with my fairly conservative views on finances.

"My father made his way to this country in 1900 as a 15-year-old emigrant from the family farm in Sweden. He worked in a furniture factory, farmed a little, decided he wanted to be a businessman, and worked his way eventually into his own store, the Broadway Grocery in Rockford. They were open from 7 in the morning until 10 at night in those days, and I literally grew up behind the counter of a grocery store and he and I have always been very close."

Look at "John B.," as his constituents call him, and, sometimes, in a flash, you can see the industrious, white-aproned grocery clerk with wavy blonde hair, who would, the customers said, amount to something one day, maybe even go to Congress. Mamie Vincer, his fifth grade teacher, disciplined him "to the notion that if you work hard and study hard you can make something of yourself," and at Rockford High the debate coach, John B. Burland, "an enormously warm and lively person," interested him in government.

He came to Washington in 1952 for the Basic Officers Training Course for the Foreign Service, and while he was preparing for assignment to West Berlin, he met the girl who was to become his wife.

"She was with the State Department, too, a clerk-stenographer; but that day there was a shortage of photographers and she was in the passport division taking pictures, and she took mine. I have always accused her of doing this by design, but somehow she took a picture with my eyes closed, and I had to go back the next day for another try. And the same girl was there – namely, the girl who is now my wife. So that kind of led from one thing to another, and we married. Our first little girl, who is now 20, was born in Berlin. In 1952 I decided to go back to the practice of law and in 1961 came here as a new Congressman. So we met here and we came back here."

Author of a book on Congress, editor of another, contributor to two others, he advocates reforming the committee system "so as to be able to deal with a growing volume and a complexity of legislation."

"The 21 standing committees really haven't changed much in the way they operate since 1964," he said. "We have a proposal that would restructure them. Instead of bills on energy and the environment being reported to one of a half dozen committees, all that legislation would funnel into one committee."

Did the Watergate revelations discourage him?

"I don't minimize the awful consequences of Watergate, but I don't think it proves the system is at fault. The results, finally, will validate the system and prove to people that the continuation of our government doesn't depend on men. It isn't just individual personalities that make this thing grow. It's the fundamental structure of the government itself — that we do have three independent branches, that we are a government of laws not of men, and that everybody has to be responsible for the law. Those are some of the basic things that, I believe, will convince people when this is all over that the system did acquit itself rather well under trying conditions."

A buzzer sounded Anderson had to go to the floor to vote. On his way out he stooped and kissed his youngest daughter asleep on a leather sofa.

"Sometimes," said Representative Anderson, "it seems that the most difficult part is trying to spend some time with my children."

"Inflation is the number one problem, and government spending, for which Congress bears responsibility, certainly comes under that head," says John B. Anderson.

Justice Douglas protects the First

On October 29, 1973 Justice William O. Douglas recorded 34 years and 196 days on the U. S. Supreme Court, a day longer than the previous record holder, Stephen J. Field, who was appointed by President Lincoln. Justice Douglas, appointed in 1939 at the age of 40 by Franklin D. Roosevelt, has spanned the tenure of five Chief Justices and his opinions appear in more than a quarter of the volumes of the Court's cases. But the performance is even more notable for quality than longevity. He has been especially zealous in protecting the individual's great protector, the First Amendment.

Born in Minnesota, he grew up in Yakima, Washington, turned to the out-of-doors to restore his strength from a childhood bout with polio; worked his way through Whitman College; came east, much of the way on a freight, and reached New York City with six cents in his pocket; finished Columbia University Law School as editor of the *Columbia Law Review,* and, after teaching there and at Yale University, moved to Washington in 1934 with the Federal Securities and Exchange Commission. In 1937 he became SEC Chairman and, in a speech that characterized his administration, denounced Wall Street's abuse of ethics. "I meant every word — every sulphurous word," he told reporters.

With the SEC he was the guardian of the independent businessman and on the bench he befriends minorities through the Bill of Rights, particularly the First Amendment: *Congress shall make no law respecting an establishment of religion, or prohibiting the free speech thereof; or abridging the freedom of speech, or of the press; or the right of the people peaceably to assemble, and to petition the government for a redress of grievances.*

In his opinion for the Court in *Terminiello v. Chicago* he wrote in 1949 that a "function of free speech under our system of government is to invite dispute. It may indeed best serve its high purpose when it induces a condition of unrest, creates dissatisfaction with conditions as they are, or even stirs people to anger. Speech is often provocative and challenging. It may strike at prejudices and preoccupations and have profound unsettling effects as it presses for acceptance of an idea . . ."

Dissenting in 1953 to *Poulos v. New Hampshire,* Justice Douglas wrote: "The command of the First Amendment . . . is that there shall be *no* law which abridges those civil rights. The matter is beyond the power of the legislature to regulate, control, or condition."

Dissenting in 1957 to *Roth v. United States,* he wrote that "Government should be concerned with antisocial conduct, not with utterances . . . The First Amendment, its terms absolute, was designed to preclude courts as well as legislators from weighing the values of speech against silence. The First Amendment puts speech in a preferred position." Freedom of expression, he reasoned, can be suppressed only when it is "so closely brigaded with illegal action as to be an inseparable part of it."

Professor L. A. Powe Jr. of the University of Texas observed in the *Columbia Law Review* of April 1974 that Justice Douglas, giving the First Amendment new dimension, would "guarantee to each person freedom of the mind, freedom of conscience, freedom of lifestyle, and freedom to expand, grow and be oneself."

In his chambers, seated at his desk under a bold red and yellow abstract painting, the white-haired Justice, with wide-set blue eyes in a face as broad as a spade, his jutting chin, the pointed end, answered questions in a soft, quick-spoken tone. One moment rough-hewn, his features softened the next with a boy-like mischievous grin, spreading across the whole rugged map, breaking it into lines of mirth.

Where would he put himself on the political spectrum — conservative, moderate, or liberal?

"Those are not very meaningful terms," he said. "I believe in rather strict construction of the Constitution, and I would think that the conservative would be one who would adhere as closely as possible to the format of the Constitution."

He was in dissent more often than his colleagues, was he not?

"Yes, they don't construe the First Amendment fully and literally. They make all sorts of exceptions that are not in the Constitution, and I don't think judges any more than lawyers or legislators should write that kind of a gloss on the Constitution. So, I'd put myself in terms of a conservative by adhering to the framework of the Constitution and leaving room for all the diversities and idiosyncracies of the individual to develop."

Among opinions he mentioned that gave him special satisfaction was the dissent of 1951 in *Dennis v. United States.* People, he said, were "led by the press to think that a group of Communists was out to overthrow the government; but the only conspiracy was an agreement to teach Karl Marx, and under our system teachers can teach anything — evolution through the Darwinian theory or the origin of life as explained in *Genesis.*

"I've also written opinions that say it's none of Government's business what a man believes. You're on the stand, you're a witness at a congressional hearing, and you believe in God. It's not the Government's business, no concern at all. If you believe in Henry George's unearned income, or in Socialism, it's none of the Government's business. Beliefs are sacrosanct, and that's a part of the great privacy of the Constitution that goes around the individual. It's the things that he *does,* his actions only, that concerns Government."

What is his feeling about the younger generation?

"The problem of man's survival lies not in conformity but in the encouragement of diversity," says Supreme Court Justice William O. Douglas.

131

"It's mixed," he said. "The pressure of materialistic standards has had a great impact. It's natural for the young man eventually to have as his goal being vice president of General Electric or what not. He's married, has a couple of kids, he has a mortgage on his house, his automobile, and life insurance premiums, and the pressures are to keep on the escalator moving up, and you can't do that if you're concerned with other problems. The corporate family is a separate, distinct unit, and nobody would ever be president of General Electric who in the 50s or 60s proposed that we recognize Peking. We standardize our thinking and set goals for these sensitive young minds to reach. The problem of man's survival lies not in conformity but in the encouragement of diversity."

What of his generation?

"I don't have much confidence in it. My generation was politically bankrupt. The only thing that we did really was to push the age of technology and science."

The nation's greatest problem, he said, was "adjusting itself to the needs of the planet rather than the continent. It's not only our problem, it's the greatest problem of the world. You see, we're short of 71 raw materials and we're desperately short of 13. In the past the industrial nations obtained their raw materials by sending their armies, and that can't be done any more in a world that is awake. And so it means the substitution of a rule of law, of working out arrangements. Summit meetings should be concerned with the hunger: Who's going to raise the food? How much can this country raise? How much can China raise? How much will we contribute to the pool? And what will we get in return? Those are complicated questions."

Is he optimistic, then, about the Republic's future?

"I'm optimistic," said Justice Douglas, "if they stick to the Constitutional requirements."

Col. Pete Dawkins aids in Defense

The car rolled to the curb and Colonel Peter Dawkins, his wife, and two children piled out, fresh from swimming at the neighborhood pool in Alexandria.

"Now it will take us 10 minutes, I'm afraid, no matter how we rush," he said, and turning to her, added: "You want to do something with your hair?"

In 10 minutes he appeared in uniform, and, even more remarkable, she in white slacks, aqua blouse, and silver necklace with turquoise stones, looked, with a silk scarf whipped around her hair, as if the Army wife had been transformed into an Indian princess.

Former All-America football player and Rhodes Scholar, Dawkins is now a White House Fellow, one of 17 among 12,000 applicants selected to work at the side of a Cabinet Secretary or White House staff member. He is administrative assistant to Deputy Defense Secretary William T. Clements Jr. "It's the art of government that one can't learn about indirectly. It's understood best by grappling with issues along with senior officials," said Dawkins.

Proposed by John Gardner out of a concern that the Federal Government was becoming distant to the American people, implemented by President Johnson in 1964, the program brings young leaders in various fields into a year's experience in the executive branch. The Fellows also travel around the United States and other countries conferring with local officials.

Dawkins was born in a Detroit suburb, attended Cranbrook School, and decided to go to West Point, although his father, a dentist, and his mother and brothers and sisters had attended the University of Michigan.

"My high school football coach, a Marine in World War II, was not a graduate of West Point, but he believed in its ideals, and then a close friend had gone there a year ahead of me and had a very happy experience, so they formed a one-two punch," he explained.

"I always liked sports," he said. "There was never a day in my childhood I didn't play in some kind of game, even if only foot soccer with a tin can and a stick."

At West Point he played ice hockey four years and captained the football team that went undefeated and wound up second in the nation behind LSU. Dawkins, at right halfback, won the Heisman and Maxwell trophies.

"My roommate used to say that I was nothing but the figment of a sports writer's imagination," said Dawkins. "That year Coach Earl Blaik came out with the Lonesome End, or the Lonely End. He attributed great significance to the difference, but I never saw it. The way it worked, a split end always stayed about 20 yards from the huddle, and because of that we became the subject of a lot of newspaper stories. My theory has always been that much of our success came because our opponents spent a great deal of time worrying about how that fellow got the signals instead of worrying about how they were going to play football against us."

Did he believe athletics prepared individuals for stressful situations?

"Yes, to the extent that it builds up a series of crisis tests. Fourth and two, on the two, a minute and quarter left in the fourth period, and you're behind six points. There's pressure there.

"In playing sports, confronting these crisis points, you are not so much overcoming your opponent as coming to grips with yourself. A lot of times you can sort of fool people – the sports writers, your opponents, even the coach on occasion, but you can't ever fool yourself; so, above all else, I think, sports enables you to know yourself, your flaws, and build up a reservoir of strength.

"But also, looking at it as I do through the experience of having seen men in combat in Vietnam,

I find that some people with the most courage are those who are not physically imposing, are not strong, sturdy guys who could play sports."

Three years as a Rhodes Scholar were valuable, he said, in permitting him to see his own country through the eyes of a sympathetic, yet critical, ally and think about his own future, which, he determined, would be with the Army.

"In many societies the military dictates values, but American military leaders have shown a special genius in moulding from this country's evolving values an effective fighting force for our national security. Ours is a derivative defense.

"Being a soldier is quite a job. You deal with destruction and a professional soldier's primary satisfaction comes from believing that the society has features about it that make investing his life in its protection worthwhile. It grows from a really abiding faith in a society, and that's what, in my judgment, lies at the heart of people who spend their lives in the service."

How did he view efforts to shape a volunteer Army?

"It's half-time. We have just finished the first full year without a draft. The numbers look very good. Four months age we were anticipating a 20,000-man short fall in the Army; we ended the year with all the services at virtually full strength. So next year will be focused on quality. Can we really attract the kinds of individuals needed for the vast range of skills in a complex organization?"

What about criticisms that the military will be populated by the poor and the black?

"A really abiding faith in a society ... lies at the heart of people who spend their lives in the service," says Colonel Peter Dawkins, White House Fellow.

"That's a proper concern. Right now I don't think the apprehension is being borne out. It's true blacks are over-represented in the sense there is now about 18 per cent of the Army black against only 13 per cent of the military age population, and I'm sure there's over-representation in terms of the lower economic groups. But I don't find that difference significant. If the military represents a genuine avenue for upward mobility, I don't see any disadvantage in its being marginally over-representative. If we can help a youngster finish high school, teach him a trade, and have him depart the Army with an employable skill, then the fact that there are more of these youths than those coming from more privileged backgrounds is a social advantage. We should make sure there aren't any glaring distortions, but right now if we prove the ability of the armed forces to impart skills and useful traits to individuals flowing through them, then I think this concern will have proved groundless."

One more question.

"Anything you want," he said. "Ask me."

But this one was for Mrs. Dawkins.

What did she see as her husband's most significant characteristic?

"Do you realize," he said, "that we're about to go on a two-week vacation and she'll have to enjoy it?"

"But I have an answer," she said. "I think he has many fine qualities, but the most valuable one is his sensitivity to other people and their needs and desires. That shows through his professional endeavors in the Army and through his friendships and through his being a husband and a father."

In the silence. Dawkins cleared his throat. "You know, of course, you're talking to one of my great fans," he said.

"Your greatest fan," she said.

Roger Mudd roams Capitol

At the close of the day-long euphoric March on Washington on August 28, 1963, Roger Mudd, who had been the CBS anchorman at the Lincoln Memorial, took the Civil Rights leaders' list of 12 demands, and, in his crisp, professional way estimated one by one their chances of passage in that congressional session. Only two, he concluded, had any chance at all.

For that analysis (which proved correct) he was criticized by Civil Rights leaders – and commended by newsmen who respect his complete honesty about himself, his profession, and the Capitol he covers.

"That was the day," Mudd remembered, "of Martin Luther King's speech. He got a cadence going – 'I have a dream!' – and the occasion was something special that helped lead to the 1964 Civil Rights bill.

"That demonstration was really feared because after the violence of the 1950s, many thought that every time Negroes marched there would be trouble, but there really wasn't that day. It was an amazing sort of outpouring.

"Congressmen didn't quite know what to do about it – didn't know whether to come down and be seen with the blacks or stay away. They weren't sure which would be more politically profitable. But after that they found it not to be politically devastating to be seen at one of those big protests.

"I discovered that the vanity of black leaders was just as great as that of the white ones. The blacks were bound together by the Civil Rights cause, but there was a lot of infighting evident that day and jockeying for position as to how prominently the speakers would be featured."

Mudd, born in the District of Columbia, graduated from Washington and Lee University, earned a master's degree in history at the University of North Carolina, taught a year at the Darlington School in Rome, Ga. His master's thesis was on the newspapers' handling of Franklin Roosevelt's brain trust, and, preparing to enlarge on it for a doctorate, he went to work for *The Richmond News Leader* to learn how a paper is put together. The newspaper's radio station, WRNL, looking for a full-time newsman, recruited him.

"The only other time I'd thought about such a career was at Washington and Lee. I was saying goodbye to one of the professors, and he said, 'You know, if you decide not to go to graduate school, you have a strong voice and you did dramatic stuff here, and so you just might think of going into broadcasting.'"

He went to CBS in Washington in 1961 and that summer was the week-end man at the White House, covering John F. Kennedy's trips to Cape Cod and Newport.

"I always felt that after a century or so of mediocrity in which whoever survived politically became President, that finally some of the things that were best for the country came together in this young man and made political life something that young men and women generally could aspire to. There were a couple of years in which politics was not looked down on; it was looked up at. Although the diplomatic area involved some drama with the missiles and Khrushchev, the legislative achievements were fairly skimpy. The real accomplishment, it seems to me, was of the spirit."

Johnson, on the other hand, compiled impressive legislative gains.

"But a lot of the bricks had been laid for Johnson's legislative wall," Mudd observed, "and he was perspicacious enough to know that he had to achieve all he could during those first two years – you know, in the name and memory of John Kennedy – and on that the Civil Rights bill,

"The spirit of reform is moving, opening up what is the people's branch to the people," says TV's Roger Mudd, who covers the Hill.

135

which had been bogged down in 1962 and 1963, began rolling.

"As interesting as the Kennedy Administration was, everything at the White House funnels through the conduit of the Presidential Press Secretary, and it's difficult to avoid elevating the President a little each time you sit down to write a piece. You wind up being a gang reporter. You can't get access to all the people you want to see.

"And so I was happy at the chance to go up to the Hill with 535 people, all of them vain to lesser and greater degrees and eager to be known. Most people on the Hill want to do a good job for their country, their state, and their district. But the big game on the Hill is to survive."

The March on Washington helped set the stage for the last major filibuster against Civil Rights, which Mudd covered daily for two months.

He succeeded, somehow, in creating suspense and a sense of action in what many Americans had considered to be nothing but political sound and fury, without substance or development.

"Each day had some little movement, some tone to it," Mudd remembered, "some coda that set it apart. The trick was to find what it was, whether a Senator's vote was softening or somebody's administrative assistant was disclosing that his Senator was ready to take a boarding-house amendment, or whatever. All those things like pick-up-sticks, formed a pattern. Only occasionally would there be a major development that we could truly say was a turning point. But every day was a little different from the one before. Some days nothing happened, but that in itself was significant."

He provided perceptive analysis of a dying political rite.

"A lot of the filibuster is designed to get the country ready for what's going to come. The politicians figured it would take a couple of months and when they heard CBS would cover it both sides were delighted. The proponents wanted to get the country ready for Civil Rights legislation and the opponents wanted to arouse their constituents against it. As a consequence both were happy to go on the tube.

"That was the last great stand of the old South. After that many of the veterans retired, were defeated, or died; and once the Senate invoked cloture on a black-white issue, the filibuster ceased to have any ammunition. Now we get little ones, for as much as a week, but then Mansfield will file a cloture petition, and on the third go-round, the Senate will shut off the filibuster."

Television is at its best at such thorough coverage, but compressing the day's news into 20 minutes at night distresses Mudd.

"The only story that you can really tell in so brief a span is when somebody dies. That takes 10 seconds, but I can't think of any other event that could be done as briefly and accurately as an obituary. Every other story requires some shading of meaning, some explanation, some accounting of motives, some background and perspective, an extra touch to let the viewer understand why the story is this way.

"More and more people in television, I believe, are concerned about the lack of time. The medium is so powerful, so effective, and hits the jugular so fast that you really need an hour every day, so that the story has some fullness."

What was his reaction to Watergate?

"The impeachment trauma has produced a more serious study of the Constitution than at any time I can remember. One benefit of the tragedy has been the growing respect and love for the Constitution. And the small step taken to televise the House Judiciary Committee's hearings may be the first step in redressing a serious imbalance between the Presidency and the Congress. It has been the President of the United States who monopolized television. It was the Congress who didn't know how to use the media. It could never speak with one voice. It was such a disparate collection of men and women. They looked kind of funny when they got on the air. But the President looked well-groomed, made up, and knew how to use the media. Now for the first time the use of the media by Congress may help make its power roughly comparable to the power of the President."

The whole scene is changing on Capitol Hill, he said. "Fresh air is finally beginning to blow through those halls up there. The spirit of reform is moving, opening up what is the people's branch to the people. They have abolished that unbelievable guide system where a citizen of the United States of America had to pay for a guided tour of his own Capitol. It was outrageous.

"In the House of Representatives there is no such thing any more as an unrecorded teller vote. Everything is recorded now. It is virtually impossible for members to hide their positions. An awareness finally has come to Capitol Hill that the Congress does belong to the people and not to the members of the Congress. And it's about time. For a branch of the government that is supposed to belong to the people, an awful lot of Congress' business is conducted in secret. But that's slowly beginning to open, and the clam shell has opened more in the last 10 years than it had in the preceding 150."

At the end of his telecast, Mudd drives to his wife and four children in their home in the Virginia countryside. Just inside the gate a weeping willow, overhanging the lane, sweeps the top of the car, and sweeps away any vexations of the day — but not his continuing concern for ample, objective coverage of Capitol and country.

The Square is a breathing space in city

Where office seekers used to flock before descending on the White House across the way, there is now a daily convening at noon, or thereabouts, of hundreds who wish merely to find their place in the sun.

136

The Washington Monument, flags dancing around its base, is a gathering place for youths whether demonstrating or celebrating. At lower right a pair clings together in fountain in the Monument area near Constitution Avenue. Diverse protests focus on the Monument, from vets denouncing war to motorcyclists opposing helmets.

A giant totem, Monument rises over youths

In sedate contrast to exuberant youths at the Washington Monument is the daily turnout of government clerks from surrounding executive offices into Lafayette Square; they loll, properly attired in tie and shirt, on the grass and share their lunches with each other and panhandling pigeons.

Egg-rolling draws throng to White House

Children congregate on the White House lawn before the South Portico to take part in the annual Easter egg-rolling contest and cheer characters from Disney films. Easter festivities began during Rutherford B. Hayes' administration. The Eisenhowers revived the custom, which had lapsed at the beginning of World War I. The public is invited — and the public, above is highly appreciative of the performance.

Pentagon, world's largest office, lies in Arlington

Five-storied, five-ringed, five-sided Pentagon is headquarters for the Department of Defense, including Army, Navy, Air Force, and Joint Chiefs of Staff.

In 1943 the Pentagon collected personnel from 17 buildings under one roof, covering more than three times the floor space of the Empire State Building.

The Living Past

Washington is speckled with memorials. Some catch the spirit of those they celebrate. Others have no more individuality than the pigeons wheeling about them. Yet in every statue there is a story.

Three that dominate the skyline – memorials to Washington, Jefferson, and Lincoln – express the traits Americans value most in their leaders: Washington, integrity; Jefferson, the free-ranging intellect; Lincoln, compassion.

The Washington Monument, known around the city simply as The Monument, rears sheer in the air 555 feet, five and one-eight inches. To stand at the base and look up is like gazing up a solid highway of masonry, narrowing as it climbs into the sky. It is a constantly changing spectacle. On a cloudy day it disappears like Jack's beanstalk into the overcast. At times, when the sky has a certain flat glare, the shaded side of the Monument seems, from afar, to be simply an aperture cut by scissors into the backdrop. When Fourth of July rockets explode around the peak, it is the tallest firecracker of all. It is a gigantic exclamation point, saying, Here am I, look! It is a tall barometer indicating the state of the atmosphere, a sundial, the thin shaft of a schoolboy's pencil, a reference point, a compass needle, an accent on every day. One looks each time in passing, for something new. Far up, at an opening in the peaked cap, there's a blue-white flash of a tourist's camera, as if the Monument winked.

It soars like a Sequoia and the tourists winding at its base in a long, never-ending line form the tap root. Around the base are planted 50 Stars and Stripes, circling the Monument as in a childhood game, whipping, straining in the wind, waving like horses' manes, rippling like running rapids, streaming red and white and a touch of blue like toy whirligigs, fragile yet imperishable, the joyful insignia of a nation that dares to be sensitive, light-hearted, open, and childlike because it is strong and unafraid.

Entering the base of the Monument, winding into it as in an ear, seeing a blank wall, tomblike, dead ahead, a girl, about 8, murmurs, "I'm scared." On the elevator's one-minute trip to the top, a taped message relates the Monument's dimensions, and at the notation that there are 898 steps, the 30 passengers look at each other and smile. As they step off the elevator, a boy tells his mother, "My ears popped!" Above them in the peak is the crisscrossed jumble of beams and trusses, the Monument's bare bones.

Two recessed windows open on each of the four sides, peep shows onto magnificent vistas: the Capitol reigning at the head of the Mall; the White House reduced by distance to an exquisite doll's house, and, next to it, the old, gray State, War, and Navy building, now sheltering Executive offices, looking with its outbreak of columns as if some mad hobbyist had turned it out with a jigsaw, decorating the facade with hundreds of spools and spindles; the snowy white temple of the Lincoln Memorial, and, finally, the dozen or more concentric circles of the Jefferson Memorial – circular walks, borders, drive, walls, colonnade, parapet, rim, brim, and surmounting all the other circles, the dome, a bull's eye.

Everything about the Monument has a touch of the fabulous, even the commission of dignitaries that oversees it. Annual meetings never varied, said one member, former Virginia Governor Colgate W. Darden Jr.

"First," he said, "we heard a report from the Interior Department that the Monument had moved two hundred thousandths of an inch, which meant it wouldn't go off balance for the next million years. Then came the report on the annual count of visitors, which always disclosed that a good many more tourists went up in the Monument than came down, at which the Commission Chairman, Earl Warren, would become terribly worked up and demand to know if any-

A strolling couple enjoys cherry blossoms around the Tidal Basin beneath the Washington Monument. Tokyo, respond

...g to interest expressed by Mrs. William Howard Taft, sent 3,000 flowering cherries in 1912. Thus the spectacle began.

body had been left up there. Interior's man would explain, patiently, that the count didn't include those who walked down the Monument's steps instead of using the elevator. Between annual meetings Warren would forget the explanation and when, alarmed all over again the next year, he raised the question, it was worth the trip to Washington to see the look of consternation that swept over the members' faces at the thought of all those people hung up there somewhere. Only inertia and God working together keep this country going."

To walk down the steps and view the 190 memorial stones contributed by states, cities, and organizations is to see American graffiti, an outpouring in stone of affection for the man, and, as well, a debate among states over the nature of the Union. Iowa, "her affections, like the rivers of her borders, flow to an inseparable Union"... Indiana "knows north, no south, nothing but the Union"... Delaware "first to adopt will be the last to desert the Constitution"...

The Southern states, on the other hand plead the Constitution as the basis for states rights: Alabama, "a Union of equality as adjusted by the Constitution"... Louisiana, "ever faithful to the Constitution and the Union"... Georgia, "the Union as it was. The Constitution as it is"...

California's testament to Washington could be a state casting its vote on the floor of a national convention for a favorite son: "California, youngest sister of the Union brings her golden tribute to the memory of the father."

The Monument towers over all, as did the man. Jefferson, urging Washington to run a second time, wrote: "The confidence of the whole union is centered in you. Your being at the helm will be more than an answer to every argument which can be used to alarm and lead the people in any quarter into violence and secession. North and South will hang together if they have you to hang on."

Plans to decorate the Monument's base twice failed, fortunately. It rises in lines as clean, straight, and true, as the lines in the character of the man it represents.

Washington said he had "no objection to any soberly or orderly person's gratifying their curiosity" by viewing Mount Vernon. They come daily in the thousands, waiting in a line that often extends from buses up the hill and through the house, a ceaseless tramping. Through it all, Mount Vernon is serene.

Plans had been that Washington would be buried in the Crypt in the Capitol, but his family decided he should rest at Mount Vernon, to which he was always trying to return. Americans regard it, more than any other of the shrines, as theirs; and that feeling is evident in the way they relax in the rockers along the broad veranda and look down the bluff at the blue Potomac River. He was, after all, the father of the country.

The Jefferson Memorial, not so successful as Washington's, is best seen from afar as from the National Airport, distance eliminating detail and leaving only the lovely curve on the horizon; or across the flat mirror of the Tidal Basin, with paddle boats plying the water, or an orchestra playing on the plaza before the portico, enlivening the mass.

The problem is that Jefferson was a word man; how do you translate the inquiring mind into stone? The architects struggled by taking his favorite form, the sphere, and repeating it, circle on circle, like a pebble dropped in a mill pond. Inside the columned, cage-like structure is a 19-foot statue of Jefferson, clad in a furlined great coat that almost skims the ground, the gift of General Thaddeus Kosciuszko.

Where the architects came closest was simply in the engraving of Jeffersonian rhetoric on walls. The guards say that sometimes visitors, standing in the Rotunda, read the words and cry.

Just below the dome, banding the Rotunda is his life rule: "I have sworn upon the altar of God eternal hostility against every form of tyranny over the mind of man."

Ranged around the wall below it are four amalgamations from his writings, including his views on slavery: "God who gave us life gave us liberty ... Indeed I tremble for my country when I reflect that God is just, that his justice cannot sleep forever. Commerce between master and slave is despotism. Nothing is more certainly written in the book of fate than that these people are to be free ..."

The other framers could rise to great utterance. Jefferson seemed to stay at that pitch. The lines spring from his correspondence, as when, writing Colonel Edward Carrington, he remarked, "If once the people become inattentive to public affairs, you and I and Congress and Assemblies, Judges, and Governors shall all become wolves."

He was happy, singing as he went about his work at Monticello, fascinated with what lay about him. Writing from Philadelphia to his daughter Martha, in December, 1790, he asked for news, and, in a phrase that seems to come from the page as a cry of ecstacy, said, "There is not a sprig of grass that shoots uninteresting to me!" He was happy because he was always creating, and the process seemed to renew rather than tire him. When John F. Kennedy brought together the Nobel Prize winners in 1962 he called the assemblage "the most extraordinary collection of talent, of human knowledge, that has ever been gathered together at the White House, with the possible exception of when Thomas Jefferson dined alone."

His Memorial is enhanced further, as, indeed, is the Federal Triangle of buildings along Constitution Avenue, by plantings of the magnolia tree, Jefferson's favorite. The magnolia has an undeserved reputation for being suffocating sweet; but the fragrance is light, if penetrating, lime-like, and the sturdy tree grows everywhere, from inner city to suburbia. The white blooms of the grandiflora, big as dinner plates, may be seen, as one early botanist noted, on a hillside a mile and a half away.

Finally the Memorial's setting is graced by a pair of mockingbirds nesting in dense shrubbery along the south wall. Jefferson prized the mocker above all other birds, and, when no one else was present, let a pet mocker fly after him about the White House. "Learn all the children to venerate it as a superior being in the form of a bird," he wrote Martha, "or as a being that will haunt them if any harm is done to itself or its eggs."

The mockingbird's flights about the Memorial are at once graceful and cumbersome. It is almost over-balanced, like a man in a frock coat walking a tightrope, by its over-long tail with its wren-like tilt. Much of the time, when flying, the bird is singing, so that flight and song all tumble together, which could account for its jerky course through the air. It may well be difficult, as with a person rubbing his stomach and patting his head, for a bird to fly and sing at the same time, especially when it's singing all the other birds' songs, too.

Mockingbirds abound around the Mall, dividing it into territories as precise as L'Enfant's grids, so that, moving from one bird's domain into another the visitor is never out of hearing of their song.

Jefferson, when the occasion demanded, blended the best of what was in the air into something better. Some critics have observed that the Declaration of Independence contains no startling new thought. Its object, said Jefferson, was "not to find out new principles or new arguments never before thought of," but "it was intended to be an expression of the American mind ..."

The mockingbird sings at all hours, even, during the seasons when it is declaring its rights, late into the night. Then, at dusk, the Jefferson Memorial, in the company of magnolias whiter than the marble walls and the mockingbird pouring out song, is at its loveliest.

Everything turned out right for the Lincoln Memorial, even the site, which, when chosen, was a swamp near the Potomac. "Don't put the memorial here, boys," pleaded House Speaker Joe Cannon. "Why, the malarial ague from these mosquitoes would shake it to pieces."

But they did. And architect Henry Bacon put the statue of a rail splitter in a Greek temple, and that worked, too. A statue by Daniel Chester French declared the nobility of the subject.

French discovered that the building, nine stories high, dwarfed an 8-foot model; he more than doubled the size of the seated figure to 19 feet. Then he badgered Congress into giving him permission and funds to light the statue properly.

At the dedication on May 30, 1922 the crowd stretched to the Washington Monument and has continued, more or less, ever since at all hours in all weathers. Abraham Lincoln, people sense, is of the people, by the people, for the people.

The Memorial is hospitable as well as awe-inspiring. Fluted columns just fit the back of a tired tourist who drops on the top step; and the steeply inclined marble bannisters, children discover daily, make an admirable slide. Inside, the visitors read silently the Second Inaugural Address's appeal for reconciliation. Then they cross the hall to the Gettysburg Address. Often, the guards say, parents read it aloud to their children. Some stand with their backs to the inscription and recite it.

What would be the odds against an address beginning four score and seven years ago ever amounting to anything? To some listening on the battlefield in Gettysburg the inauspicious start must have seemed the beginning of an unwitting parody of the worst in speeches; but then, almost before they caught the solemn import of what he had been saying, Lincoln was finishing with the assurance "that government of the people, by the people, for the people shall not perish from the earth."

Walt Whitman, wandering around Washington, standing on the fringes and penetrating with a poet's eye to the heart of things, saw Lincoln returning from the Second Inaugural on March 4, 1865 looking "very much worn and tired; the lines indeed of vast responsibilities, intricate questions of demands of life and death, cut deeper than ever upon his dark brown face; yet all the old goodness, tenderness, sadness, and canny shrewdness was underneath the furrows."

About that time Lincoln was telling friends he was so weary that rest "seems never to reach the *tired* spot."

To a crowd massed at the White House on April 11, two days after Robert E. Lee had surrendered at Appomattox, Lincoln made his last speech. In nearly a cajoling tone he tried to relieve the war's bitterness in the minds of his hearers, treating the Confederate states as if, instead of former foes, they were returning prodical sons to be met with rejoicing and complete forgiveness.

"Finding themselves safely at home, it would be utterly immaterial whether they had ever been abroad," he said. "Let us all join in doing the acts necessary to restoring the proper practical relations between those states and the Union, and each forever after, innocently indulge his own opinion whether, in doing the acts, he brought

People come at all hours in all weathers to look at the heroic sculpture of Abraham Lincoln. The colossal seated s

e, measuring 19 feet in height, is made of 28 marble blocks fitted so perfectly they seem to be one block of marble.

the states from without into the Union, or only gave them proper assistance, they never having been out of it."

The imagery, delicately and strongly wrought, showed again Lincoln's understanding that "reconstruction is more difficult and dangerous than construction or destruction."

At the least, had he lived, he would have blunted the radical's repressive measures. At the most, following the line of Northern philanthropists who established colleges for blacks, Lincoln, moving in his patient, selfless, enduring way, might have made it possible for the Federal Government to assist blacks in overcoming the deficits of 250 years of slavery. Considering the regenerative effect of the Marshall Plan to Western Europe, even modest assistance to the Southern states, if nothing more than support of education for the blacks, would have hastened and eased the reconstruction that was still going on 100 years later.

A boy when Jefferson was alive, Lincoln was a throwback to the Founders. Washington, the Adamses, Jefferson, Madison, and Mason used to speak of the Republic as if it were a child or a sweetheart and threw everything in the scale to save it. The pledge of life, fortune and sacred honor was no empty phrase — most of them died bankrupt — and Lincoln was with them in his faith in the Declaration of Independence and his determination to save the Union at any cost.

At the Cabinet meeting on April 14, 1865, the last day of his life, he remarked that, fortunately, Congress had adjourned "and there are none of the disturbing elements of that body to hinder and embarrass us" in the first efforts to animate the states. He studied pictures of Lee. It was a good face, he remarked.

He and his wife had an engagement for the theater that night, but he didn't feel like going, and if it were not for disappointing so many people, he wouldn't. But, as he nearly always did, he surrendered to other's needs. Generally, he enjoyed the theater as a chance to be alone and yet to be with people, free for a moment from favor-seekers. Hidden in the Presidential box, he could let his mind slip free and range. So much had been done, so much remained to do.

In the box that night, noting that the young couple with them, Major Rathbone and Miss Harris, had clasped hands, Lincoln took Mary Todd Lincoln's hand. She bridled and asked what Miss Harris would think of "my hanging on to you?" And he, eyes on the stage, said mildly she'd think nothing about it.

Among other trials, he'd had to deal with his wife's mental instability. His father had once said, when you make a bad bargain, hold to it all the tighter. Lincoln held her hand, and they watched the play. Once or twice, as he leaned forward in the box, the audience in Ford's Theatre saw the droll, sad face. John Wilkes Booth, an actor who had easy access to the theater, slipped into the President's box and shot him.

Lincoln was carried across the street to the home of William Petersen, a tailor. What impress visitors today is the place's melancholy aspect. It was a house prepared for woe — beige wallpaper, glistening black horsehair sofa and chairs, cramped quarters — even before it received the dying President. The back room where Lincoln died is so small that the bed was angled in the room and Lincoln had to be angled on the bed. Surveying the bed, a woman tourist exclaimed, indignantly, "Abraham Lincoln was a tall-l-l man and that bed looks mighty small." On the bedstand's mottled marble top is a wash bowl and pitcher. On the wall are engravings of Bosa Bonheur's "Horse Fair" and "The Village Smithy."

After lingering through the night, Lincoln died in the rainy spring morning.

"Now he belongs to the ages," said Secretary of War Stanton.

In Richmond, Robert E. Lee said, "This is the hardest blow the South has yet received."

In front of the Treasury building is a statue to Alexander Hamilton, who put the country's fiscal structure on a sound basis. A slight figure he was a fighter of tempered steel and during the Revolution won the sobriquet of the "Little Lion." He was George Washington's principal confidential adviser, his "writing and riding" aide. As was true with most of the men who fought in the Revolution with Washington and saw the states' disarray, Hamilton advocated a strong central government. He and Jefferson were bitter foes, but when the election for President was stalemated in the House of Representatives, between Jefferson and Aaron Burr, Hamilton begged his followers to reject Burr and vote for Jefferson.

In Virginia, Arlington County is the home of the Marine Barracks, oldest post in the Corps. The Barracks stages a resplendent Sunset Parade each Tuesday during the summer months before the gigantic Marine War Memorial, a representation in bronze of Joe Rosenthal's photograph depicting Marines raising the Stars and Stripes over Iwo Jima on February 23, 1945.

Two companies of Marines in dark blue tunics and the red-jacketed U.S. Marine Drum and Bugle Corps come marching on two sides from behind the gargantuan statuary, like toy soldiers appearing from a box, file on file, the precise squares of men descending the Memorial steps in such unison that their ranks seem smoothly flowing tank treads.

The drum and bugle corps has every brass instrument known to man and drums galore, the drummers' hands flailing the snares, the

Lincoln Memorial offers Gettysburg Address

On November 19, 1863 Abraham Lincoln delivered on the battlefield of Gettysburg an address that lasted only a few minutes and forever. Now visitors to his Memorial often read it aloud, softly.

FOUR SCORE AND SEVEN YEARS
AGO OUR FATHERS BROUGHT FORTH
ON THIS CONTINENT A NEW NATION
CONCEIVED IN LIBERTY AND DEDICA-
TED TO THE PROPOSITION THAT ALL
MEN ARE CREATED EQUAL ·

NOW WE ARE ENGAGED IN A GREAT
CIVIL WAR TESTING WHETHER THAT
NATION OR ANY NATION SO CON~
CEIVED AND SO DEDICATED CAN LONG
ENDURE · WE ARE MET ON A GREAT
BATTLEFIELD OF THAT WAR · WE HAVE
COME TO DEDICATE A PORTION OF
THAT FIELD AS A FINAL RESTING
PLACE FOR THOSE WHO HERE GAVE
THEIR LIVES THAT THAT NATION
MIGHT LIVE · IT IS ALTOGETHER FIT-
TING AND PROPER THAT WE SHOULD
DO THIS · BUT IN A LARGER SENSE
WE CAN NOT DEDICATE~WE CAN NOT
CONSECRATE~WE CAN NOT HALLOW~
THIS GROUND · THE BRAVE MEN LIV~
ING AND DEAD WHO STRUGGLED HERE
HAVE CONSECRATED IT FAR ABOVE
OUR POOR POWER TO ADD OR DETRACT ·
THE WORLD WILL LITTLE NOTE NOR
LONG REMEMBER WHAT WE SAY HERE
BUT IT CAN NEVER FORGET WHAT THEY
DID HERE · IT IS FOR US THE LIVING
RATHER TO BE DEDICATED HERE TO
THE UNFINISHED WORK WHICH THEY
WHO FOUGHT HERE HAVE THUS FAR
SO NOBLY ADVANCED · IT IS RATHER FOR
US TO BE HERE DEDICATED TO THE
GREAT TASK REMAINING BEFORE US~
THAT FROM THESE HONORED DEAD
WE TAKE INCREASED DEVOTION TO
THAT CAUSE FOR WHICH THEY GAVE THE
LAST FULL MEASURE OF DEVOTION~
THAT WE HERE HIGHLY RESOLVE THAT
THESE DEAD SHALL NOT HAVE DIED IN
VAIN~THAT THIS NATION UNDER GOD
SHALL HAVE A NEW BIRTH OF FREEDOM~
AND THAT GOVERNMENT OF THE PEOPLE
BY THE PEOPLE FOR THE PEOPLE SHALL
NOT PERISH FROM THE EARTH ·

Lincoln's life pervades Washington

At 511 Tenth Street, N.W. is Ford's Theatre, left, where on April 14, 1865 actor John Wilkes Booth shot the President while Lincoln was watching a play. Across the street at 516 is the house where he died. In Ford's basement is a museum of 4,000 items.

After the Capitol, the Lincoln Memorial, below, is the most popular attraction in Washington. Architect Henry Bacon created a white marble temple with 36 fluted columns representing the states in the Union at the time of Lincoln's death.

Daniel Chester French designed a seated Lincoln eight feet high but after he saw a model of the statue in the huge Memorial, he more than doubled the size to 19 feet on an 11-foot pedestal. French worked seven years for funds and approval to perfect the lighting.

153

Beyond Washington's expressways and boulevards the Lincoln Memorial shines, a block of light, through the nigh

alling poet Walt Whitman's description of him: "a star in steadfast purity of purpose and service and he abides."

Arlington ceremony honors Chief Justice

At Arlington National Cemetery, the country's leaders gather, below, on July 12, 1974 for the burial of Earl Warren. An honor guard, right, salutes the Chief Justice. A soldier, below, paces his solitary guard of honor before the Tomb of the Unknown Soldier.

The view, right, from the Custis-Lee Mansion overlooking Arlington National Cemetery is magnificent, starting with visitors gathered at the grave of John F. Kennedy, looking across the ranks of white headstones to the Memorial Bridge and to the Lincoln Memorial.

158

The graves of the Kennedy brothers, side by side in Arlington National Cemetery, draw people in an unending procession. They pause, above, at the cross marking the grave of U.S. Senator Robert F. Kennedy, A visitor, left, takes a picture of others viewing the grave of President John F. Kennedy. The hillside setting, designed by John Carl Warnecke, has a white marble terrace, granite rectangle, and eternal flame.

Visitors pause at the Kennedy grave sites in Arlington

Theater-goers at the John F. Kennedy Center for the Performing Arts throng the Grand Foyer which traverses the length of the 630-foot building. Dominant note in the huge hall is the sculptured head.

Artist Robert Berks made the heroic likeness of the President. The Center honoring him has four major facilities: an Opera House, a Concert Hall, the Eisenhower Theatre and a Film Theatre.

Kennedy head distinguishes Grand Foyer

sticks moving blurred as dragon flies' wings. At one point a master drummer, stepping from the ranks, tends at once to three bass drums held by his colleagues, a performance to make Tom Sawyer pale with envy. A dozen flashing cymbals catch the sun's rays. Throughout, there's smartness in each man's step and the hint of a swagger in the swinging right arm. At the head of all is the high flying flag, furling and unfurling red, white, and blue at its own sweet pace, a majestic slow-swimming swan. The brass plays marches, the bold slant strokes of the National Anthem, and the sweetness of "My Country, t'is of thee," the national hymn that undid us when, hearing it in church on the Sunday after the President's assassination, we opened our mouths to sing and nothing came, except sobs.

On the brow of Arlington Cemetery is the Custis-Lee Mansion, where the master of the house, Robert E. Lee, struggled over the choice of whether to accept command of the Union troops or go with Virginia. He left Arlington forever, and his decision to lead the Army of Northern Virginia prolonged the Civil War three years. Outnumbered usually 2-to-1, Lee divided his forces daringly and defeated one Union general after another. Finally Lincoln found Grant, who would match Lee's hammer blows, and Sherman who demonstrated that war was hell, if he didn't say it, by sweeping like a scythe through Georgia and the Carolinas.

Slavery's shadow had fallen across the country's history from its birth. European immigrants arriving in New York turned west and developed that bread basket rather than compete with the South's slave labor. At Lincoln's call, they came east and the North's vastly superior manpower and industrial production wore down the South. At Appomattox, Lee's battalions were so shrunken that their battleflags were massed like a color guard.

After the war, rejecting handsome offers, Lee accepted the presidency of Washington College in Lexington, Virginia. (The trustees borrowed the suit their emissary wore to extend the bid to Lee – and then borrowed $1,500 for the General's salary.)

At Washington and Lee University they tell this story. A veteran came slowly up the walk toward the President's house. Lee left company to go greet him. The two talked a while, and then the General reached in his pocket, gave the veteran money, and bade him goodbye. He rejoined his friends, and one asked to what company the veteran had belonged in the Army of Northern Virginia. "Oh", said Lee, "he was on the other side."

In 1864 the U.S. Government refused payment of taxes on Arlington from an agent of Mrs. Lee's, confiscated the estate, and set aside 200

Contrasting statues populate the capital

President Theodore Roosevelt, above left, raises his hand over the Potomac island dedicated to his memory. Below left, General William T. Sherman towers over his Square. In a grove, right, in Rock Creek Cemetery is the shrouded bronze figure created by Auguste St. Gaudens as a memorial to the wife of Henry Adams. Mark Twain called the statue „Grief." But Adams called it "The Peace of God."

From atop the Washington Monument a view of the Jefferson Memorial in its lovely setting by the Tidal Basi

...scloses ring after ring — circular walks, borders, drive, colonade, brim, dome — in the design by John Russell Pope.

acres as a military cemetery. After the war, through a Supreme Court decision, Custis Lee, the General's son, regained title to the property and sold it in 1883 to the Government for $150,000. Additional purchases enlarged the cemetery to 420 acres.

The Arlington Memorial Bridge, symbolizing the reuniting of North and South, connects the Lincoln Memorial with Lee's home.

Hugging the hillside below the Custis-Lee Mansion is the grave site of President Kennedy. On a curving slant, wall are inscribed quotations from the President's speeches. Visitors approach along a granite walkway from the road below, a pulsating current of human beings, a living, moving freize, reading the words on the wall, standing in loose array, tall-stalked flowers, at the grave site of field stone, moving on to pause at the cross nearby marking his brother Robert's grave.

Simplicity, as simple as Taps, is Arlington's keynote. The Tomb of the Unknown Soldier is a single 50-ton block of white marble, and, pacing the guard of honor, a solitary soldier. Chief Justice Earl Warren, General John J. Pershing, President William Howard Taft, and Secretary of State John Foster Dulles rest there.

The simple, white headstones sweep the green hills, through sun and shade, white as dogwood petals in the spring, white as snow in the winter, looking from a distance, year-round, like a white tufted bed spread, carefully tucked at the headboards, with the prayer, "Now I lay me down to sleep, I pray . . ."

Across a causeway over the Potomac River, just off George Washington Memorial Parkway, one reaches Theodore Roosevelt Island, an 88-acre sanctuary within sight of the gleaming glass cliffs of Virginia's vest-pocket cities.

An association bought the island in 1931 and gave it to the Federal Government in the memory of the 26th President. On the crest is a paved plaza, surrounded by a moat, and featuring a 17-foot bronze statue of Roosevelt, backed by a 30-foot granite slab. Four 20-foot tablets bear quotations from his speeches. Roosevelt is depicted with right hand raised high, as though ready to bring it sweeping down into the left hand with a resounding smack. At such a moment the President would roar, "I hate the man who skins the land!"

Coming upon the statue through the trees is like bumping into the Jolly Green Giant. Time should enhance the resemblance with a fine, green patina. The sentiments engraved on the slabs reflect his forthright approach to obstacles and the enthusiasm with which he went about creating the U.S. Forest Service, five national parks, and numerous wildlife refuges.

166

At ease on the plaza before the Jefferson Memorial some enjoy the concert while others roam about the site. There is much to see. On the pediment over the portico the figure of Jefferson stands before the committee named to write the Declaration of Independence. Inside the Rotunda is the 19-foot statue of Jefferson in a fur-collared great coat given him by Kosciuszko.

Concerts blend sculptural and musical beauty at Memorial

A view of the West Mall captures three basic designs: the sleek, whale-like contour of a jet plane from Nationa

rport, soft clusters of cherry blossoms around the Tidal Basin, and the classic dome of the Jefferson Memorial.

169

The island is the thing. Children, let loose, run the trails, not satisfied, any more than Robinson Crusoe, Huck Finn, or Jim Hawkins, until they have circled their new-found kingdom. Leaving the trail, picking a way long the river bank over fallen trees and through screens of saplings, it is even possible, as the traffic's roar subsides and the bird cries dominate the woods, to feel a little lost on Theodore Roosevelt Island in the heart of metropolitan Washington.

On the causeway a youth, getting ready to fish, was in such a hurry to wet his line that he didn't even look up from baiting the hook. A clerk in the District Office, he had slipped down during his lunch hour, he explained, head bent, and the river looked good and so, after work, he had come directly with his tackle. (Washington probably has more fishermen than any other city with a population exceeding 700,000. When herring run in early spring, fishermen are as numerous as the rocks in the Potomac.)

The youth made a cast. "I guess they had several million dollars to blow," he said, "but it would have been simpler just to have rented paddle boats to those who wanted to get onto the island."

Roosevelt's reaction to that, no doubt, would have been "Bully!"

Facing Pennsylvania Avenue in a grassy triangle in front of the Archives building is a marble block engraved; "In Memory of Franklin Delano Roosevelt, 1882–1945."

Talking with Justice Frankfurter in the White House, FDR designated the spot and said of the memorial, "I should like it to consist of a block about the size of this –" and he put his hand on the desk. "I don't care what it is made of: whether limestone or granite or whatnot, but I want it to be plain, without any ornamentation, with the simple carving 'In Memory of ...'"

In the early 1960s there was a move to place a memorial to Roosevelt near those of Jefferson and Lincoln. The design would have featured a statue among towering slabs, like dominos, carved with Rooseveltian quotations. But FDR had made it plain that he wanted his memorial plain, and so it remains.

The roof of the John F. Kennedy Center for the Performing Arts shelters the Opera House seating 2,200, the Concert Hall, 2,700, the Eisenhower Theatre, 1,100, the Film Theatre, and three restaurants. Necessarily the roof is large. It would cover four football fields. The Center is similar in shape and dimensions to a nuclear aircraft carrier. From its promenade deck, 12 stories up, the sightseer feels like he is a Pueblo Indian scouting Washington.

The Center's local point is a huge bronze head of John F. Kennedy, sculptured by Robert Berks, based on a life-size model he created in

Statues honor leaders who left legacies

Bronze statuary, right, honors Mary McLeod Bethune, educator. It is the first memorial to a black and a woman in Washington. Mrs. Bethune hands two children her legacy of love, learning, and dignity. Cedar Hill, below, was the home of Frederick Douglass in his last years. Born a slave near Easton, Maryland, he became an abolitionist newspaperman and orator.

MARY McLEOD BETHUNE
1875 · 1955

A statue of John Marshall, fourth and greatest Chief Justice of the U.S. Supreme Court, graces the Capitol's West Front. The bronze was done by W.W. Story, son of Marshall's colleague, Justice Joseph Story.

The vivid red-jacketed U.S. Marine Drum and Bugle Corps high-steps in the Sunset Parade at the Marine Corps Wa

Memorial north of Arlington National Cemetery. Blue-coated companies from Marine Barracks also pass in review.

Statues salute three soldiers of two wars

In Sheridan Circle Union leader Phil Sheridan perpetually reins his great horse and exhorts his retreating troops to turn back to Winchester. Gutzon Borglum's statue captures vigor of horse and rider. In Lafayette Square, right, portly General von Steuben seems to be reviewing troops he drilled for Washington and General Rochambeau points to Executive Offices. In DuPont Circle, below, people simply relax.

the week following the President's assassination. A viewer's impulse is to reach out and touch the rough-textured, broken surface of the face. It is whole and yet wounded.

What he had tried to catch, said the sculptor, was the conflicting sense of the President's youth and hope and the unfulfilled promise. In a technique developed through 400 works in more than 20 years, "the final outside texture happens as the first clay is put on the foundation," said Berks.

Berks also sculptured the statue of Mary McLeod Bethune in Lincoln Park, the first memorial to a Black American or to a woman on public land in Washington. She combined the creased face of a matriarch with the jaunty air of a field marshal. The 15th of 17 children born to former slaves in Maysville, S. C. she scrapped for her own education and then for that of her race. She founded Bethune-Cookman College in Daytona, Fla., organized the National Council of Negro Women, and for 20 years in Washington advised four Presidents. She was jobfinder, counseler and mother to a host of youths, many of whom attended the dedication of the statue July 10, 1974.

It depicts Mrs. Bethune handing to two children the legacy she wrote for her race. Its key sentences are engraved on the base: „I leave you love . . . I leave you hope . . . I leave you a thirst for education . . . I leave you the challenge of developing confidence in one another . . . I leave you a respect for the use of power . . . I leave you faith . . . I leave you racial dignity . . . I leave you a desire to live harmoniously with your fellow man . . . I leave you, finally, a responsibility to our young people."

Frederick Douglass, black orator, abolitionist, and antislavery editor, was born to a slave family in Easton, Maryland. He spent his later years in Washington at Cedar Hill, now preserved as a shrine. In 1852, addressing the Ladies Anti-Slavery Society in Rochester, N. Y., he made his own declaration of independence: "What to the American slave is your Fourth of July? I answer, a day that reveals to him, more than all other days of the year, the gross injustice and cruelty to which he is the constant victim. To him your celebration is a sham.

"I am not included in the pale of this anniversary. This Fourth of July is yours, not mine. You may rejoice. I must mourn. Do you mean, citizens, to mock me by inviting me here today? There is not a nation on earth more guilty of shocking practices than America at this very hour."

Depicted at ease in a low-slung chair, a book in his lap, a statue of John Marshall, his back to the Capitol's West Front, looks benignly down Constitution Avenue toward the Monument of his old Commander-in-Chief.

Fourth and greatest Chief Justice of the U. S. Supreme Court, Marshall, a rangy, dark-eyed Virginia frontiersman, fought in the Revolution's

Children frolic on the lawn of George Washington's Mount Vernon, America's most celebrated home and one th

176

...he American people feel is peculiarly their own. *"No estate,"* said Washington, *"is more pleasantly situated than this."*

Washington's Mount Vernon is restful

Sightseers relax, above left and below, on Mount Vernon's broad veranda overlooking the placid Potomac. They inspect, above right, the dependences at the home's west entrance. Others gather, next page, before the ivy-covered brick tomb of George and Martha Washington. He gained title to Mount Vernon after the death of his half-brother Lawrence and expanded it greatly.

On a clear day from the steps of the Lincoln Memorial the view looking east to the Washington Monument make

quite plain that the capital of the United States of America is "of the people, by the people, for the people."

Let the country's glorious Fourth ever be celebrated with illuminations, said John Adams. No show can outshir

Fourth of July fireworks bursting in the sky over the memorials to the framers and saviors of the Republic.

battles, and bore Valley Forges rigors, and emerged with rank of Captain and the conviction that a strong central government was vital to the country's survival. "I went into the Army a Virginian, I came out an American," said Marshall.

He was a quick-witted, winsome person who could see straight to the heart of a court case or a jest. In a Philadelphia club where he was visiting, the members were playing a game in which they proposed a word to be used in verse. Somebody tossed Marshall "paradox." Gazing reflectively toward the bar, which was lined with whiskey-swigging Kentuckians, Marshall responded:

In the bluegrass regions of Kentucky,
A Paradox was born.
The corn was full of kernels
And the Colonels full of corn.

He loved to play horseshoes at his home of Richmond; idolized his invalid wife and took her out of town to escape the noise of the Fourth of July; and as fast as Jefferson, his kinsman and foe, appointed members to the Court, won them to his own way of thinking. The sculptor of the statue, W. W. Story, was the son of a Jefferson appointee, Justice Joseph Story, who became a Marshall protege.

John Randolph of Roanoke, who seldom had a good word to say for anybody, labeled a bundle of letters from Marshall "That master of the human heart."

In the case of *Marbury v. Madison* in 1803, Marshall's opinion confirmed the Court's authority to review acts of Congress and find them invalid under the Constitution. "It is," he said "emphatically the province and duty of the judicial department to say what the law is." A legislative act contrary to the Constitution "is not law ... It is a proposition too plain to be contested ... there is no middle ground ... the Constitution is superior to any ordinary act of the legislature."

John Adams, who nominated Marshall Chief Justice, said, "My gift of John Marshall to the people of the United States was the proudest act of my life."

In following the law the Justices frequently go against the Presidents who appointed them. President Eisenhower used to say that changes in the hearts of men would bring about desegregation, but his appointee, Chief Justice Earl Warren, brought in the Court's ananimous ruling that it would come abouth with all deliberate speed under law.

And in *Baker v. Carr*, establishing one man-one vote, Chief Justice Warren said, "We are cautioned about the dangers of entering the political thicket ... Our answer is this: A denial of constitutionally protected rights demands judicial protection; our oath and our office requires no less of us."

It all stems from the man whose statue looks with benign eye down Constitution Avenue.

When a public figure lacks a memorial in Washington, he always can be shuffled off onto one of the government buildings coming along. The assignment of James Madison to the third unit in the Library of Congress is apt. Madison's first move on undertaking a project was to read every book about it on which he could lay his hands. Preparing for the Federal Constitutional Convention of 1787, Madison wrote Thomas Jefferson in France and requested "whatever may throw light on the general constitution," and Jefferson, delighted when someone asked for information, responded with 100 books.

Madison was a small, slight figure, "a withered little apple-John," wrote Washington Irving; "no bigger than half a piece of soap," said another contemporary. Yet when his associates looked into the intent blue eyes and felt the workings of the incisive mind, the adjective "great" occured to them. The bounteous Dolley, at the start of their courtship, coupled the two adjectives when she noted that "the great little Madison" was coming to call. Jefferson called him "the greatest man in the world." Jefferson's way was to think of an idea and then leave the enactment to Madison, as with his Virginia Statute for Religious Freedom. Patrick Henry, who hated Jefferson, said he could "forgive anything else in Jefferson but his corrupting Mr. Madison." (There is no public memorial in Washington to the Revolution's foremost orator, which would not fret Henry. Having helped overthrow British rule, Henry detected "an awful squinting toward monarchy" in the Philadelphia convention's document. A states righter, he was the most popular figure in Virginia in his day and this, which would have sufficed for him.)

At the Federal Convention Madison sat in front of the presiding member and took notes on every speech, a task, he said later, that almost killed him. With his habitual precision, he objected to being called the "Father of the Constitution," which was not "the off-spring of a single brain but the work of many heads and many hands."

Nothing underscores more dramatically the value of dissent and discussion than the 55 delegates framing the Constitution, everybody putting in his bit. The seed of the Convention's "Great Compromise" – the decision to allot seats in the House of Representatives on population and give each state two Senators – was planted by Roger Sherman.

Madison, though no orator, was an enormously persuasive speaker. In the Virginia Convention to ratify the Constitution in 1789, he would take the floor after Patrick Henry's thundering and, speaking quietly as if some thought had just come to mind, holding his hat before him, look casually in the crown – which contained his notes, carefully prepared.

When he left the White House, Woodrow Wilson retired to a four-story, red brick, Georgian-styled house at 2340 S Street, N. W., where he lived for three years until his death in 1924.

It contains, among other items, the brass shell which held the first shot fired by American troops in

The John F. Kennedy Center for the Performing Arts stretches in the night, like a shining teahouse, 630 feet. The top

...eck, 12 stories high, offers a magnificent view of downtown Washington, the great memorials, and the Potomac River.

World War I. Wilson's aim was to make the last shot fired in that war the final one anywhere. If that seems idealistic, Wilson's contention was; "The world is run by ideals. Only a fool thinks otherwise."

Greatness hopped, skipped, and jumped down the centuries from the founding fathers to Wilson. Throughout – as President of Princeton University, trying to establish the tutorial system and abolish clubs: as reform Governor of New Jersey; as President championing a "New Freedom" for the common man and small business; as international diplomat urging the right of self-determination for nations – he shared with the Revolutionary War leaders a concern for the individual.

After World War I he wrested major concessions from the Old World leaders, only to see the Versailles Treaty with the Covenant of the League of Nations endangered in the U. S. Senate. To rally public support he set out on a cross-country speaking tour. "I do not hesitate to say," he warned, "that the war we have just been through, though it was shot through with terror of every kind, is not to be compared with the war we would have to face next time. What the Germans used were toys compared with what would be used next time."

In the midst of a speech on September 25, 1919 at Pueblo, he suffered a stroke. With his collapse went any hope of compromise with Senate opposition. The League lost by seven votes.

In 1961 President Kennedy appointed a commission to create a memorial for Wilson. Meanwhile, the setting for his grave is appropriate.

As planes approach the capital, passengers see on the northwest horizon the thrusting gray-brown bulk of the Washington Cathedral, resting, a beached Ark 70 years a building on the city's highest rise, awaiting, great bays open, the onrolling thunder of a gathering spiritual storm.

In the Cathedral, amid carvings symbolic of his life, is the tomb of Woodrow Wilson. Atop the tomb rests a crusader's sword.

Washington's town square is Lafayette Square, across Pennsylvania Avenue from the White House. Statues at the four corners show the foreign accent in the American Revolution. The park, of course, is named for the young Marquis de Lafayette, who contributed his dash and a substantial amount of cash to the American cause. He returned in 1824 for a farewell tour that lasted a year and throughout addressed his frenzied audiences as "we Americans." He died in 1835. His grave was covered with earth from Bunker Hill.

Sharing the square with him are Thaddeus Kosciuszko, the Polish general; Comte de Rochambeau, commander of the French Army in America, and Baron von Steuben, the inspector general of the Continental Army, who drilled the troops into shape at Valley Forge. Holding center stage in the Square is General Andrew Jackson on a horse as spirited, which seems to be rocking.

The Square, taken as a whole, is itself a memorial, and well deserving of the adjective living, since it is filled usually with tourists and, at lunch, by executive office clerks. It also has been a gathering place for protesters and parade watchers.

Among its memorable moments was the crowd that gathered there to watch the arrival of Nikita Khrushchev at Blair House, the nation's official guest residence, in September 15, 1959. Along the parade route down Pennsylvania Avenue there was a mild ripple of handclapping, aimed at President Eisenhower, squeezed in the back seat of a convertible between the Soviet Premier and Mrs. Khrushchev.

Ike received rousing ovations in his life but none more heart-felt than the very cautious applause sent his way that day. It was the sort you give someone for whom you care very much when it would not be proper to show unrestrained approval, a restrained of flick of the wrist, a surreptious salute to a member of the family during a pressured moment.

The crowd showed its deep feeling after the President had deposited his guest, carefully like a man putting down a precious vase, and started back across the street to the White House.

Then all 10,000 packed in Lafayette Square, unleashed their emotions, and gave Eisenhower a roaring full-throated, prolonged cheer, the sort the home team gets when it runs on the field for a championship game. Ike looked startled then flashed an unabashed grin.

At 10th Street, where Pennsylvania Avenue intersects D. Street, is a statue of Benjamin Franklin, with, generally, one or more pigeons perched upon it or swirling about like Gentle Ben's aphorisms. He is blissfully unaware of the new FBI Building advancing behind him with juggernaut tread and frowning cope.

In their deliberations the founding fathers relied on portly Franklin as a pillow, a buffer in debate, who knew exactly when to lighten the charged atmosphere with a story or call for a prayer or engage in what must have been the first mild filibusters while everybody got his temper. He also knew the importance of the right finishing touch.

When the delegates to the Philadelphia convention concluded their making of a Constitution, Franklin made his inimitable verbal signature.

"Whilst the last members were signing it," reported Madison, "Doctr. Franklin looking towards the Presidents chair, at the back of which a rising sun happend to be painted, observed to a few members near him, that painters had found it difficult to distinguish in their art a rising from a setting sun ... I have, said he, often and often in the course of the session, and the vicissitudes of my hopes and fears as to its issue, looked at that behind the President without being able to tell whether it was rising or setting: But now at length I have the happiness to know that it is a rising and not a setting sun."

Wonders on the Mall

In spring, 1974 an academic procession of black gowned scholars with vivid splashes of color on their shoulders, like red-winged blackbirds and Baltimore orioles, picked its way from the Folger Library to the grand West Front of the Capitol.

The procession marked the 600th anniversary of the death of the poet Petrarch, who forwarded the Renaissance that arrived in America in the person of Thomas Jefferson.

The ceremonies on the West Front included a speech by Rhode Island Senator John Pastore, who read excerpts from an address that Petrarch had delivered on the Capitoline Hill in Rome.The week-long celebration signaled that Washington itself is experiencing a flowering of the arts, at a much greater rate, indeed, than New York City.

On the Mall the National Gallery of Art has built a magnificent new wing, and the Smithsonian Institution has created the Joseph H. Hirschhorn Museum and Sculpture Garden, which looks, refreshingly, as if it were dropped from an angel food cake mould in a sand pile. It will house a treasure of 6,000 art objects many of the caliber of Rodin's "The Burghers of Calais."

Not only are fabulous museums breaking, brilliant crocuses, into view, but established institutions are putting forth green shoots. The Folger, housing the world's most extensive collection of Shakespeareana, now has a repertory company presenting plays in its Elizabethan Theatre and sending programs through the public schools. No point, said Folger Director O.B. Hardison, in having a theater without plays.

The Corcoran Gallery of Art's new chairman of trustees, Lloyd Kreeger, has announced plans to reinvigorate that venerable institution. Those who cherish its objects need no stimulus to drop by and see, for instance, "The Turkey," a tar-dark bronze by John Singer Sargent, the epitome of all turkeys, a monstrous clump of dark feathers, sturdy as a stump, head slung back, strutting.

Nor does one need a push to visit, periodically, the Phillips Collection for the bracing tonic of viewing El Greco's "The Repentant Peter," raising soulful, suffering eyes, clasping his hands in anguish, a twisted, tormented form, and, turning from that exercise in agony, to see Pierre Auguste Renoir's summery, sumptuous, sensuous "The Luncheon of the Boating Party."

At the Smithsonian's new Renwick Gallery, concentrating on design, one finds the metamorphosis of the telephone from the practicable hand crank variety on the wall to a pastel kidney one holds to the ear. Within a tribal shout of the Capitol is the new Museum of African Art in a row house once occupied by Frederick Douglass. The Smithsonian dusted off its National Collection of Fine Arts and housed it in the queenly old Patent Building along with the National Portrait Gallery. The Portrait Gallery includes likenesses of each President and two of Lyndon Johnson, who said that his first one was "the ugliest thing I ever saw." In the Freer Gallery is a world of oriental art and Whistler's famous "Peacock Room," in which one feels he has been clapped into a green lacquered box.

And, of course, the drama is flourishing, with the Sylvan Theater in the park beneath the Washington Monument, the restored Ford Theater, the Washington Cathedral, Wolf Trap Farm, the lovely, Arena Stage, and numerous private and academic productions. A cultural center had been envisioned for Washington more than 150 years. Finally, September 2, 1958, President Eisenhower signed the National Cultural Center Act that fostered the Kennedy Center, a renaissance in itself. The National Symphony Orchestra has advanced to the front rank of the nation's symphonies. The cultural explosion, with good things raining around Washington, could be summarized by the motto over the Folger's exhibition hall. "I shower a welcome on ye; welcome all."

The droll, red "Castle on the Mall," the original Smithsonian Institution building completed in 1855, has grown

one of the most endearing edifices in a complex of nearly a dozen museums. It still is a haunt of owls and scholars.

Washington's museums show a rich trove

"Aphrodite," above, by Antonio Cavona, stands in the Corcoran Gallery's Rotunda. Humble tourist, left, bows to Bodhisattva, 7th century A.D. Chinese, in the Freer Gallery

Renwick Gallery, above, is a showcase for design and crafts. Note how the neighboring building for the government's executive offices has been styled to blend with the Renwick. In the Phillips Collection, far left, visitors relax beneath Renoir's "The Luncheon of the Boating Party." The entrance of the National Collection of Fine Arts features "Belleraphon taming Pegasus" by Jacques Lipchitz.

Smithsonian presents many, varied faces

On a hot day the fountain on Constitution Avenue outside the Smithsonian's Museum of History and Technology lures crowds. Next door, right, patrons depart from a fountain of knowledge, the gigantic National Museum of Natural History.

The Smithsonian Institution, a complex of 11 museums and art galleries, was established in 1846. It owes its origin to James Smithson, an Englishman, who bequeathed half a million dollars to the United States for the increase of knowledge.

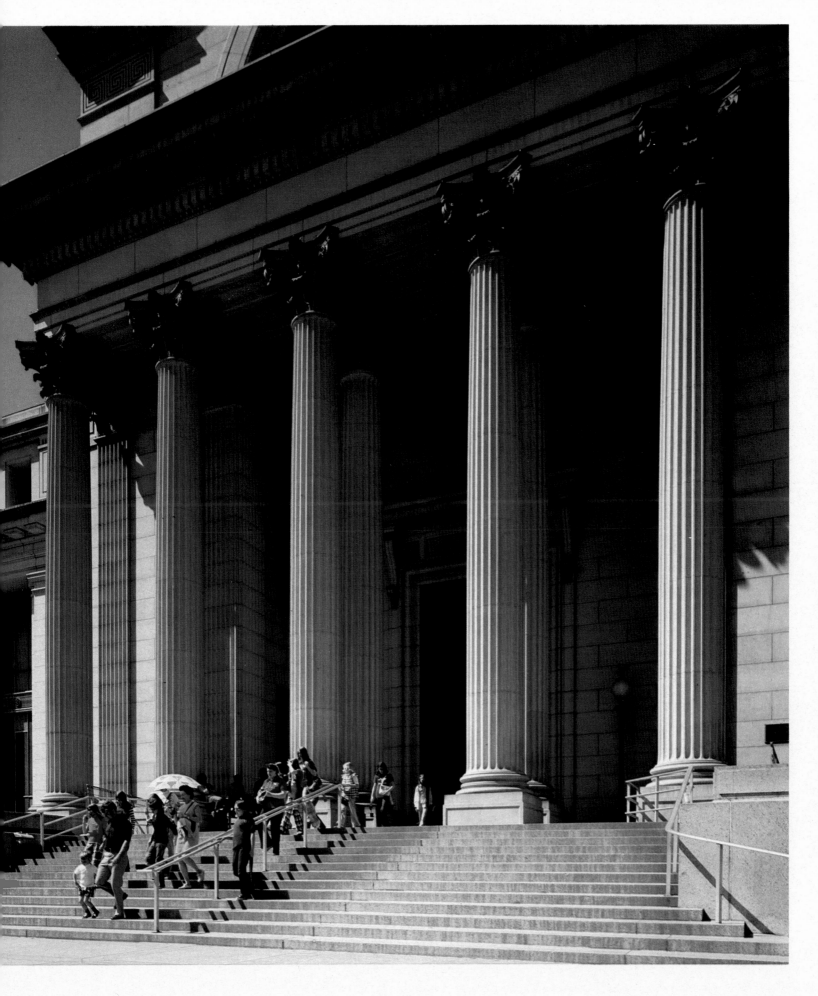

*A pair of rapt connois-
seurs, right, swap
opinions about a painting
of Diana by Auguste
Renoir. Another Diana,
right below, a sculpture by
Jean-Louis Lamoyne, is
the subject of careful
study by a fellow artist.
Meanwhile, "The
Return of the Prodigal
Son" by Bartolome
Esteban Murillo, below, is
not welcomed with wild
excitement by somebody's
young son gazing
abstractedly across his
knees into infinity.*

196

In Peter Paul Rubens' fine painting of "Daniel in the Lions' Den", above, 11 lions occupy the canvas with Daniel. The sumptuous work, a gift of the Ailsa Mellon Bruce Fund, covers nearly an entire wall. Andrew W. Mellon, former Secretary of the Treasury, funded construction of the National Gallery and gave it his fabulous collection. Opened in 1941, it is the largest marble structure in the world and extends 780 feet.

National Gallery of Art offers riches

The Smithsonian with headquarters in the redstone Castle on the Mall, grew from a bequest by wealthy James Smithson, Englishman, who had never seen America but must have sensed that fame for him lay in the New World. Generally called eccentric, he deserves to be termed visionary. When he died in Italy, he left more than $500,000 "to found at Washington, under the name of the Smithsonian Institution, an Establishment for the increase and diffusion of knowledge."

In the mid-1960s the Smithsonian began increasing and diffusing itself at a splendid rate reminiscent of Francis Bacon's announcement: "I have taken all knowledge for my province."

The Smithsonian, often called "the nation's attic," is a little sensitive about the nickname. And in the sense that attics are cluttered, musty, and so low-beamed as to knock one's nogging, the term no longer applies. The exhibits at the Museum of History and Technology, for instance, are presented with such verve that a turn through the galleries is like walking through the nation's history with a subtle guide pointing out the highlights. It is still, however, an attic in the sense that the visitor makes exciting discoveries of clothes and objects used by ancestors. What one sees first in History and Technology is the Star-Spangled Banner, not just any flag, but *the* Star-Spangled Banner that moved Francis Scott Key to write the poem that became the National Anthem.

And no wonder he saw it. As one sings the anthem, one sees a modest 6 foot by 3 foot flag flying in the dawn's early light over Fort McHenry. But Key need not have raised the question of whether it could be seen. Hanging, stripes down, the flag is as big as an inverted billboard, and the visitor is likely to take it for a gigantic mural. It measures 30 by 34 feet, but it is displayed against backing fabric that shows its original 42-foot length before souvenir hunters cut off swatches.

Wandering through History and Technology, one hears, unbelievably, the fast, imperative ding-ding-ding of a train, the sound of a genuine steam locomotive pulling into the station, and for a moment the surface under foot seems gritty and life revolves again around the depot, going down in the morning and afternoon to see if there's mail and watch who gets on and off and wish one were getting on, and the politician saying, when asked to commit himself to a probable candidate, "I don't buy a ticket until I hear the whistle blow." In the mind's eye soot-stained arches rise overhead and dull green benches carved with initials swim into focus.

Pursuing the entrancing sounds the railroad buff, anybody 40 and over, comes upon a showroom filled with a 280-ton Pacific-type passenger engine – the 1401 – that formerly ran on the Southern. Its great, green, gleaming length is embellished with bold yellow lettering and scrollwork.

The monumental National Gallery of Art lures visitors to see one of the world's greatest collections of paintings, sculptu

d graphic arts and offers as well a magnificent backdrop on the Mall for someone who sits in quiet, pensive repose.

Paul Mellon shares art

There was, Paul Mellon remarked, looking around, "a kind of mixture of things" in his office as chairman of the board of the National Gallery of Art. The mixture from his private collection consisted of paintings by Whistler and Bellows and sculpture by Gericault and Eakins.

Mellon delivers quiet understatements in a drawl, flavored by the English accent acquired in his childhood — his mother was English — and at Clare College Cambridge studying for an honors degree in history. Earlier he was graduated from Yale University.

"Do you want my glasses on or off?" he asked the photographer. "When I go to the races I take them off because I'm looking through binoculars most of the time and then if we win a race, I leave them off because I forget to put them on again, and so my picture is usually taken that way at the races. I like those pictures a little better."

Pictures are frequent of such Rokeby Stables winners as Quadrangle, Key to the Mint, and Arts and Letters. ("Part of the fun of having horses," he once said, "has to do with naming them.") Dry humor, directed usually at himself, runs through his conversation. He has a receptive, listening face and steady, blue eyes.

When he was in college in England he became interested in sporting books and sporting artists and bought his first painting, a portrait by George Stubbs of a horse named Pumpkin. His father, Andrew W. Mellon, "had paintings all around the house," Mellon noted. "He told me stories about them and why he liked them. And my sister Ailsa, too. Don't forget her. She was equally interested in the Gallery. All her collection of French paintings is here. Also, she and I have more or less jointly underwritten the new building."

The new east building has 590,000 square feet, 70,000 more square feet than the Gallery built by Andrew Mellon, an expansion, it was noted, which no doubt would please the father. "It would, it would," agreed Mellon.

"My father didn't preach about it," said Mellon. "but in an indirect way made it plain that people who have money have an obligation to use it wisely."

Strolling through the Gallery, he paused before Cezanne's "The Artists' Father," which he bought and gave to the Gallery because he thought it belonged there. Looking at the whites, grays, and beiges in the portrait of an old man reading a paper, Mellon observed that it pleased him "because of its tranquility and homeyness."

An expression of amusement crossed his face as he said, "When I gave that picture to the Gallery we had a press conference with Director Carter Brown and myself with the painting and one of the newspaper people figured that the reason I liked the picture was because Cezanne's father looked like me!"

He stopped before a lovely painting. "There's a funny story about that picture," he said. "My sister always had a hard time making up her mind about anything but particularly about buying art. The dealer had been keeping this for her about two years. He showed it to me one day, and I said not to tell Ailsa I was interested in it. 'Let her make up her own mind about it,' I said, 'but if she doesn't want it, I'll take it.' I knew that if he told her I wanted it, she probably would buy it immediately. Eventually, after about another year, she did."

Noticing that a visitor to the Gallery was hesitant to walk between him and the photographer, Mellon raised his hand to halt the picture and stepped aside quickly. His thoughts, giving the way to a visitor or giving a gallery to a nation, tend to be for others.

The thoughtfulness marks his infrequent appearances in public. Arriving for induction in the Army six months before Pearl Harbor, Mellon, stepping from a bus in Richmond, was asked by newsmen why he at 34 was volunteering when deferment age was 28. "Because I thought it was the right thing for me, personally, to do," he said quietly. In the Army he taught horsemanship and supervised a stable of 80 horses at the Cavalry School at Fort Riley, Kansas and then went overseas with the OSS to train French sabotage and intelligence agents. On returning to civilian life he showed a growing concern for unobtrusive public service over private business.

He and his wife live near Washington on a 5,000 acre farm in Virginia, a one-story country house that rambles along a swell of ground. "It sort of grew," said Mellon. Screened by plantings and walls, the house, like the owner, extends in many directions, and is as self-effacing.

In the Gallery Mellon showed, with boyish enthusiasm, a model of the new building.

The National Gallery of Art needed more space because of steadily increasing attendance and a collection that had expanded from Andrew Mellon's nucleus of 121 paintings to more than 30,000 works of art. The board also decided to establish a Center for Advanced Study in the Visual Arts.

The new building's site was a trapezoidal plot of land where Pennsylvania Avenue and the Mall converged in front of the Capitol. Architect I.M. Pei solved the problem of the site's awkward shape by designing two triangles — the larger for the exhibition gallery and the other for the Study Center — joined by a triangular skylit court.

Walking back through the galleries to his office, Mellon passed a class of excited school children gathered around a painting. "That," he said, "is the greatest sight of all."

"My father . . . . in an indirect way made it plain that people who have money have an obligation to use it wisely," says Paul Mellon, chairman of the National Gallery of Art.

201

Catherine Shouse guides Wolf Trap

Near Vienna, Virginia, 14 miles from Washington, D. C. on a site where settlers used to trap wolves for bounties, is a national park for the performing arts, Wolf Trap Farm, the first and only one of its kind.

It now is a kind of trap for people, luring them from such far-flung points as Abilene, Texas and Boise, Idaho, for an evening with the likes of the Bolshoi Ballet, the Metropolitan Opera, or marathon performance of Bach.

Dominating the 100-acre park is the Filene Center, a 10-story tall concert hall.

Of natural Oregon cedar mellowing to an orange-brown, the Center is a show in itself, in which, if the show on stage should pall, one's mind can roam.

Supporting the Center's roof and opening the auditorium to the out-of-doors on both sides are huge louvers, like great columns in a redwood forest. Seen segmented between the 10-story tall louvers the foliage outside forms elegant streamers of green tapestries. Night breezes and sounds sweep through the hall. A mockingbird joins the National Symphony Orchestra. A bob white's piercing call punctuates a musical tribute to Thoreau.

The Center, about the color of a bass viol, is like another magnificent musical instrument; and, at the same time, reminds visitors of the bandstands of their youth, attics in which they rummaged for costumes, carousels, park pavilions, and even, at the sight of people hurrying up the long green slope from the parking lot, of Shakespeare's "Wooden O," a theater drawing spectators like bees to a hive.

It seats 3,500, and another 3,000 can lounge on the hillside at the rear of the center, a natural amphitheater with a clear view of the 100-foot stage.

Wolf Trap's moving spirit, Catherine Filene Shouse, observed that young couples don't bother about baby sitters; they just bring along a picnic supper in one basket and a baby in another, and enjoy the show. "The babies never cry," she said. "I've never heard a baby cry at Wolf Trap."

(They cry all right, but the sound outdoors mingles with the sawing of cicadas, fades under the stars, and goes unnoticed.)

A tall, regal woman with white hair and shrewd, blue eyes, Mrs. Shouse bought Wolf Trap Farm in 1930 while living in Georgetown "to give my children a chance such as I had while growing up in Boston to know soil, trees, and animals so that by learning their demands they might better understand and guide their own lives.

"Now this park is about the only bit of green grass left out here for people to enjoy," she said. "I've always been interested in the performing arts and the land; and I didn't want the land that we and our friends had enjoyed to be subdivided."

She gave the U. S. Department of Interior 100 acres and funds to construct Filene Center, and persuaded the American University to train youths in music, drama, and dance.

Congress accepted the gifts in 1966. An early-morning fire damaged 60 per cent of the nearly completed building in mid-March, 1971, but Mrs. Shouse said, "No use looking back. We have to look ahead and get ready!"

The Center opened on schedule July 1, last-minute banging backstage mingling with the strains of the orchestra warming up "Mefistofele."

The Center is named for her parents, Mr. and Mrs. Lincoln Filene of Boston. Her childhood home was a center for musicians and educators. Her mother, believing music should be a part of everybody's life, sponsored lessons for poor children in a Boston settlement house. Her father, grandson of the founder of Filene's specialty store, was interested in education.

"Our house in the country was a mecca for professors who would come down and talk over ideas with a businessman. My father's feeling was that business and education shouldn't be so far apart. So, as we children were growing up, people of many interests were in our house, and naturally we became engaged in what was going on in the world."

While she was still in prep school at Bradford, Massachusetts, Woodrow Wilson's campaign excited her, and she staged rallies in the school gymnasium and organized the town for him.

In 1917 and 1918, at Wheaton College, she persuaded the administration to let her invite youths from colleges and universities east of the Mississippi to discuss job opportunities for women graduates — conferences that led to the formation of the Intercollegiate Vocational Guidance Association.

With the outbreak of World War I she convinced her family that "if I'd been a boy, I'd have been in military service, and so I took a war job in Washington with the Department of Labor — assistant to the chief of the Women's Division of the U. S. Employment Service. My assignment was to recruit women for war industries and open employment offices. I was 21 and I was traveling about five nights a week — yes, I was born in 1896, I'm the oldest living graduate around here of anything — and then after the armistice I stayed in Washington to study Negro employment."

She went to Harvard, became the first woman to accept a degree there, a masters in education, and wrote a book on job opportunities for women with a high school education.

She was cofounder of a research organization, the Institute of Women's Professional Relations — which sponsored studies between 1929 and 1945 and fostered in 1942 a conference on War Demands for Trained Personnel.

"DuPont technicians, I remember, were saying that they

couldn't use women in their laboratories because of the smells, and someone at the conference arose and said, 'What about cabbage in the kitchen?' — and that was a new idea!"

After her campus campaign for President Wilson, she represented Massachusetts on the Democratic National Committee and took part in politics until she married Jouett Shouse, who was then Chairman of the Executive Committee of the Democratic National Committee.

Spinoffs from Wolf Trap produce other good causes. An enrichment program, conducted by the National Park Service, introduces culturally deprived pupils from Washington's public schools to Wolf Trap. More than 80 per cent of the children return with their parents.

The Wolf Trap Company gives 60 youths, recruited from colleges in all sections of the Country, ten weeks of intensive training as a bridge between the classroom and the demands of the stage. Among planned facilities is a year-round theater for conferences and drama.

Each Fourth of July Wolf Trap presents an all-day program of jazz, band, and symphony music and fireworks. "While one of the concerts was going on," said Mrs. Shouse, "I looked out from the ramp of the second story balcony, and I could see children playing ball and throwing frisbies on the grounds and directly below two different groups of adults were sitting there playing cards and listening to the concerts. It was an active, happy crowd but a quiet one, and it was very heart-warming."

"I've always been interested in the performing arts and the land; and I didn't want the land we had enjoyed to be subdivided," says Catherine Shouse, Wolf Trap's donor.

203

Mary McGrory lights The Star-News

Long after midnight in the air-conditioned chill of a cavernous hotel basement partitioned by draperies into press rooms, a tousleheaded young woman huddled over a typewriter, still looking for just the right word to evoke the mood and thrust of that day's Presidential nominating convention.

"That was me," said Mary McGrory. "Can you explain it to me? Can you help me? I'm always hoping I'll meet somebody who'll say, well, your problem is thus and so."

But next day the syndicated column ran smoothly, one vivid phrase into another; and newspapermen, reading with envy, wondered how McGrory does it.

"You know what I do? I re-write so often I leave things out. I mean, a genuine incompetent after all these years – no facility, basically no idea of how to go about it, still! It's like a pick axe, and you have this great big stone, and you're hacking away at it and hoping that somewhere inside there is something."

Her slightly slant eyes are touched with rue, her mouth with humor, and her voice, reflective and melancholy, rises and falls, in a lulling chant, except for the wit that flashes through the commentary. Some columnists flinch when writing critically of sources; McGrory's pick axe is unsparing.

"I don't have any sources. That's why I have to go and see it myself; not in the investigative sense, but just to look and listen."

She came from the *Boston Herald* to the *Washington Star-News* as an editorial assistant. "I read galleys and wrote letters and visited the composing room and answered the telephones, and I can do shorthand and typing. I hate to brag, but I can."

She also wrote book reviews, and after seven years the *Star-News* turned her loose on the McCarthy hearings. Readers rejoiced at the coverage.

When did she first realize she wanted to write?

"I still don't want to."

Did someone in her childhood do a lot of reading?

"My father read all the time. He grew up in South Weymouth, Massachusetts, where there were very cold winters and very little recreation, and he was the best Latin scholar they ever had at South Weymouth High School. The summer before he was to go to Dartmouth on a scholarship, his father died; and he, being the eldest of eight, was expected to go to work, which he did. He was very fortunate in that he got a civil service job at the Post Office. He never complained. And so, he was a reader."

At the Girls Latin School in Boston she contributed to the *Jabberwock*, the school magazine, and at Emmanuel College, edited the yearbook, and, still reading, began reviewing books for the *Boston Herald*.

"I like going around, and I like talking to people," she said. "I like hearings. And I am crazy about courts, crazy about courts. Nobody makes speeches. Nobody tells you the story of his life. Nobody tells the witness that he's the greatest man he's ever seen. There's a kind of antiseptic, fair quality about the courts. I mean Gerhard Gesell is the nearest thing to absolutely arbitrary power I've ever seen. I guess I have a little of the absolutist in me, but we're not going to talk about that today.

"Political conventions are too big for me. It's the same as I am about shopping. I'm always sure when I go into the store that somewhere in the back room is the dress I want. When I go to conventions, I'm thinking, at this moment somebody is getting the *unadulterated* word from the nominee, and here I am stuck in the South Dakota delegation.

"My paranoia is really rampant. It's the shopping syndrome completely activated. I know – and very frequently it's the case – that Dave Broder or Evans and Novak are at that moment in a room having a friendly drink with the candidate, who is telling them

everything," Mary McGrory said.

What person in public life impressed her most?

"I guess Adlai Stevenson. I heard that acceptance speech in 1952 and I can't tell you the gratitude I felt for the generosity of ideas, the lucidity of phrasing. My brother and I were listening in New Hampshire at 2 o'clock in the morning, and he said, 'Supposing Daddy could have heard?'

"Then in 1954, trailing around after him, I asked if I could see him. A look of pain crossed his face. He had to write. I would just get these glimpses of him – it was on the train – and he would be going over every syllable and crossing out words. Of course, I understood perfectly well, so I just followed him around and wrote a couple of pieces about him. They apparently were called to his attention, and so when we met again over the centerpiece of some political banquet, he said, 'I read your stories and found them bewitching.' I had never heard a politician use that word before."

Did she agree with Democratic Majority Leader Mike Mansfield's estimate that John F. Kennedy might have become a great President?

"I'm not sure. I don't know. There was a sort of civility he brought and a regard for other people's opinions, and I think that was very valuable."

John Gardner of Common Cause had said that Vietnam obscured President Lyndon Johnson's progressive domestic record.

"Yes, I think that what he did with civil rights is forgotten really. I think he was swamped by the Kennedy advisers. He was so conscious of the love for Kennedy that he wanted to preserve everything, and he didn't ask those questions about Vietnam that he should have asked. He challenged everybody else. He was afraid of their hard and shining Yankee certitudes. He was

undone by those people in the sort of psychic sense. They were so alien to him, and he knew they had been around this magical figure."

What was her forecast for the country?

"When I read the framers of the Constitution and their exhilarating talk of liberties and the people's genius, I'm hopeful. Recently we seemed to have lost that spirit. Perhaps it was the corruption of the war. People got the idea they couldn't do anything about it and that others knew more than they did. The colonists didn't think anybody knew more than they did. They also thought their opinion was worth as much as others'."

How did she regard Washington, D.C.?

"It's full of transients, of opportunists who come here to get something — reputation, money, power, whatever. It's not a city in the way of Boston, where everybody has deep roots and an emotional commitment to place. It's a big motel. And we are all passing through. I like it because it's transient and temporary. But you spend half your life saying goodbye to people."

And hello?

"Yes. But more goodbyes than hello, somehow."

"And I love the greens of Washington. Oh, it's lovely. And I have a garden."

What did she raise?

"Flowers, and not very well. Shasta daisies and ageratum. My grandfather, who was born in Ireland, was a gardener in Boston for one of the great shoe magnates. My father was a mad gardener, but I never paid much attention, and then it suddenly came over me. In the blood."

"When I read the framers of the Constitution, and their exhilarating talk of liberties . . . I'm hopeful," says Mary McGrory, columnist for The Washington Star-News.

205

Meg Greenfield writes editorials

The door to the Georgetown house was opened by green-eyed Meg Greenfield, looking like a heroine from one of Shakespeare's light-hearted plays: pert, mirthful, witty. Her voice, moreover, is husky and comradely, and if that combination doesn't carry the day, her laugh will.

The petite deputy editor of the *Washington Post's* editorial page and nine other writers make a conning tower of the ivory tower. At the breakfast table Washington is well posted. (And at the dinner table the vigorous *Washington Star-News* lights the way.)

Miss Greenfield, born in Seattle, attended Smith College, studied abroad, did research for Adlai Stevenson's 1956 Presidential campaign, reported for the *Reporter Magazine*, and joined the *Post* editorial page in 1968 at the invitation of editorial page editor Philip Geyelin.

"And I love it," she said. "I love the paper. I love the people."

What did she find satisfying about editorial writing?

"It imposes a kind of restraint and responsibility. You are taking the paper with you where you go, and it's not a place for flights of fancy. What I like is that you are near the news and yet a little bit off it, trying to figure what it meant, not what's going to happen tomorrow."

And what is an editorial page's purpose?

"It's first purpose is to put events in the news section into some sort of perspective. A reader often has the news coming at him fast, and our role is to try to see what's important and suggest what it means.

"And since we are in Washington we serve, whether we want to or not, as an instrument of communication among people in government. The guy may open his paper and read that a House committee has reported a bill, affecting him, that he never heard of before.

"It has terrible occupational hazards – pomposity and stri-dency. Phil and I have a parody sentence we use – 'It is past time for men of good will to cease the bootless acrimony' – when either of us lapses into editorialese.

"Also, there's an abiding danger that if editorial writers are not careful they convey a sense of arrogance and super-ciliousness. Sometimes I look down the page and think, well, there was every reason we wrote each of these editorials; and yet a reader, turning to them over his morning coffee is entitled to say 'What is this voice that's telling me with such certainty who's right and who's wrong?' I think it's important to try to convey some awareness that you may not, in fact, know everything.

"We all work well together because some of us tend very quickly and clearly to say this is good and that is bad, but others of us, are inclined to say, wait a minute, and so there's a kind of dynamic there."

For relaxation she gardens, and reads medieval history and modern mystery novels.

"In the evening I like to read things that have nothing to do with what we are going to be discussing in the next day's editorial conference. It's a kind of escapist approach with history. Anything after the 13th century is getting too close.

"In mysteries I prefer Nero Wolfe. When I find one of those, I'm fairly unreachable until I've finished it."

Had she met Adlai Stevenson in the 1956 campaign?

"Once, when I was chosen one of eight young women to march as a little honor guard with him through a gigantic rally in New York City. I can still remember ... We all walked out ahead smiling with our name tags, and the mob broke loose – they all wanted to shake his hand – and we joined arms in a kind of flying wedge. I'm not anybody's idea of a very good bodyguard, and we were all bobbing about, and Stevenson who, whatever his other gifts, just was not good with crowds, was appalled. People were pushing us, and we were weaving around, and Stevenson kept sticking his hand between two of us to shake hands with someone else, with this look of 'Get me out of here!' And he kept trying to shake my hand, and after about the third time. I remember saying, 'Governor, I'm part of the par-ty!' It was very Adlai; he just was not a politician."

Throughout her remarks on editorial writing a theme was the necessity for balance and judgment and taking the job, but not oneself, seriously. Had that view been shaped in childhood?

"I expect so. My mother died when I was a child, and some women relatives wanted to take me and my brother, but our father wouldn't have it, and that was kind of great.

"It was a very practical jokey kind of household with a series of housekeepers who couldn't quite believe this whole situation. I was the sort of serious student of the family, which my brother and father found at once desirable and kind of funny, so there was a lot of teasing about that. You weren't ever allowed to take yourself too seriously.

"Once I was going to England for a year to study William Blake, of whom they had never heard and refused to concede was important. They had a big farewell party for me, and afterwards I got on a train going across the country, with a steamer trunk and dreams of Blake, and sat in the compartment thinking, in a glow, of this great adventure, and when I went into the bathroom of that compartment, what did I see but a gigantic horseshoe of dead flowers – who knows how long they had been up to it, all those drooping flowers – the biggest horseshoe of dead flowers you ever saw, framing the john, with a gold ribbon across it and in big letters: 'THANKS FOR EVERYTHING, MEG! .... WILLIAM BLAKE.' That's sort of where I came from."

"A reader often has the news coming at him fast, and our role is to try to see what's important and suggest what it means," says Meg Greenfield, editor.

207

Dillon Ripley directs Castle

How appropriate that the Smithsonian Institution should be headed by an egghead! And how fortunate for that rare breed to have so warm a representative in a high place.

S. Dillon Ripley—balding, tall, angular—appears slightly forbidding while flying, abstract in thought, along a corridor, but when he focuses on the person before him, his face breaks into an engaging grin. Further, his enthusiasm for the project at hand, whether the launching of the *Smithsonian* magazine or the introduction of barn owls into a tower of the Castle on the Mall, is infectious.

Once, long ago, owls had nested in the red towers poking above the green mall, and Ripley, out of love of tradition and birds, resettled them there.

"We kept a pair a year at our zoo," he said, "and then we put them in the loft. Volunteers fed them every day and gradually the female showed signs of wanting to nest. We fed them three months, until they had well-grown young, and then we opened the windows, and they have been seen flying in and out, with things in their claws."

Tourists?

"No, mice and rats that follow the tourists who leave bits of sandwiches in the bins around the Mall. So we have a ready supply of food for the barn owls, who are happily at home. It's an amusing sidelight to life in the Castle."

He has opened quarters in the Smithsonian to the owls' human counterparts, scholars in the Woodrow Wilson School of International Studies, and thus, as new buildings arise to house exhibitions, he is restoring the administration headquarters to its old role as an academic cloister.

His love of learning probably traces to childhood illnesses when his mother read Shakespeare to him. His interest in birds was whetted by an Episcopalian minister who took the boys in the boarding school at Southboro, Massachusetts on bird hikes. "I was so interested he made me chairman of the Bird Bath Committee," he said.

At 13, visiting India with his family, he went with his sister on a walking tour into western Tibet, "about which I'd been reading since I was seven." After graduating from St. Paul's School and Yale University and graduate studies in zoology, Dr. Ripley in 1936 joined a zoological expedition to New Guinea, and has been doing field work ever since in the Far East. In 1943 he received a Ph. D. degree from Harvard. Even with the OSS in Asia during World War II, he managed to observe birds – and also met and later married Mary Moncrieffe Livingston, who shares his enthusiasms, collecting insects while he studies birds. They have three children.

In 1964, after 18 years on the Yale University faculty and four years as Director of Yale's Peabody Museum of Natural History, he became the Smithsonian's eighth Secretary.

"When I was a graduate student at Harvard," he said, "there were two kinds of biologists, those who stayed in the laboratory and if a field mouse ran across the window sill would not look at it because it was not a controlled experiment; and there were others, across the street in the museum, who wouldn't look at the field mouse because it wasn't skinned and stuffed. And I, who was interested in the behavior of living birds, fell somewhere in between. So with me museum work has been an exciting avocation tied into my professional love, research and field work on the life history of birds."

He is optimistic about the Smithsonian's future, "which means, of course, I'm optimistic about the future of the increasing diffusion of knowledge among men. The Smithsonian has the potential to become the national leader in conservation of objects made by man, and I hope that we will be one of the leaders in the inevitable necessity for conservation thinking in our use of objects made by nature."

Does he feel Washington must be consigned to crime, poverty, and mediocrity?

"Those things are sort of day-to-day, but I discern encouraging long-range changes, such as the heightened anticipation and awareness of people. Although our educational system appears to be deteriorating, opportunities both in education and the community's surrounding cultural assets continue to develop excitement in young people. And so people are getting better educated en masse even though perhaps individually they are not getting as good an education. It's an anomaly, but I find more curiosity among young people today that I did when I was young. Perhaps in my youth there were more channelized methods of communication and ways of creating excitement.

"I am not convinced that our education system today is as good as it should be. And I am convinced that sociologists are wrong in their aims that education must be adapted in a totally egalitarian way so that nobody will be able to leap ahead. I cannot believe that our civilization is going to succeed if we say we must graduate everybody at the same level and cut back those in whom, as the spacemen say, all systems are go. You can't really stop such a child, anyway, once he gets going.

"To return to Washington, it's a beautiful city and has a tremendous potential for style and quality in everyday living, and it has glamor."

Is he optimistic about the United States?

"Yes, we are still by far the most well-situated of nations in terms of our people, our average rate of intelligence, our skills, our technological innovativeness. These, plus the rationale and realization of our pluralistic faith, can keep us together."

"The Smithsonian has the potential to become the national leader in conservation of objects made by man," says Dillon Ripley, Secretary of the Smithsonian Institution.

Roberta Flack teaches in song

The first time ever you hear her voice, you wonder that the mellow contralto under such perfect control can sound so free and easy, taking long phrases without any hint of effort, flowing naturally, meticulous, yet melodious; thoroughly trained, yet warm and spontaneous.

The artist with the soulful voice, Roberta Flack, entered the far end of the long room as if she were alone. Stooping in a white gown to put a tape deck in the player, she looked for an instant like a child dressed to play "Grown Girls" and then, straightening as the music started, she came forward smiling, holding out her hand.

Roberta Flack, who now lives in Alexandria, Virginia, moved with her family from Asheville, North Carolina to Arlington when she was 5, went to public schools there and in Washington, D. C., and entered Howard University with a scholarship.

"We had a very close household," she said. "My father, a draftsman, worked with the Veterans Administration. He was an excellent cook, a great pastry man. I remember that because as a little girl that's what I liked best."

She had learned, she said, to appreciate his culinary skill all the more since she had the chance to travel and sample the cooking of fine chefs in other countries.

"I just marvel at what a really fine cook my father was," she said.

"My mother played the piano and organ for the Methodist Church and as a little girl on Sundays I sat at the organ beside her. My interest in music, I suppose, began there. I started studying piano formally at 9.

"I finished high school at 15, young in experience as well as years. Nearly all my childhood had been in a totally black community. At the end of my junior year, I did go in the summer to Hood College as a representative of the Negro chapter of the Junior Red Cross. That was the first time I'd been around students my age

of another race. It was a very rewarding educational situation. I made many friends and cemented my love for people.

"I'm weak for people, anyway. Most persons, I believe, have the same basic quality to be good, no matter what their color. Recently Hood College gave me an honorary degree, and I was touched that they remembered one of those young people they had helped.

"At Howard I majored in piano for two years and then switched to music education because it became clear that black concert artists had few opportunities to perform, much less make money. Two of my teachers, Hazel Harrison and Vivian Scott, were gifted concert artists, and Hazel was an expert on Bach, but few people knew her name."

After graduation from Howerd she studied a semester with Emerson Meyers at Catholic University. When her father died, she took a job teaching in a black high school in Farmville, N. C. Talking of teaching, her voice quickened until the words tumbled impetuously.

"They hired me as a vocal music teacher, but there was no money for that in the budget—the general assumption is that black people can sing and dance naturally — so I taught three classes math, one English, and everybody music.

"In the South there's enthusiastic interest in choral music. Black students look forward to being judged every year in contests with their peers, and my principal and the superintendent wanted their students to have that experience.

"I crammed so much music down their throats you couldn't believe it. And they loved it! When they were picking tobacco all day and couldn't come to school, they still managed to make it to rehearsals. Among 1,300 students were some who were handicapped and mentally retarded. I taught them with all

the others. That was a deep lesson for a 19-year-old girl. To be a teacher is to be a student. I grew up that year."

She taught seven years in Washington at three junior high schools. The "most exciting and challenging student body," she said, was at Bannaker Junior High in the inner city.

"The kids were hard to control, but it was my job to try, and I loved it and them. I used to tell them: 'I'm a musician, not a muhjician!'"

"They gave me all kinds to teach—bad and good ones, honor students, borderline cases — but everybody can appreciate music. Some went only to my class, and I spent much time teaching them to read. That kind gets very bored and impatient unless they realize some little success every day. It's important that they feel: 'I've done something.' Sometimes just to master three or four words was an achievement."

While teaching she substituted one night for her own music teacher who played the piano at the Tivoli Opera Restaurant in Georgetown. In 1968 she gave up teaching and began singing at Mr. Henry's on Capitol Hill.

"In the audience were Congressmen and their families, and during the long Sunday brunches, you couldn't get near the place. It was great," she remembered.

"I used to do some protest songs, and customers would come to me and say, 'You sang that song with so much love.' I've had people — white and black, some of whom thought they'd never touch someone of another race — standing in the aisle and holding on to one another."

"Music is terribly underrated as a way to communicate. It's perhaps the greatest. People all over the world understand the message, even if there are no words."

From an album recorded in 1969 came her first hit, *The First Time Ever I Saw Your Face.* "I didn't know anything then about the record business, but I knew

that song was good, I could sing it three or four times, and the audience would ask to hear it again. That's how it all started."

The hits continue to come regularly: *Killing Me Softly, Jesse Come Home,* and *I Feel Like Making Love.*

Her voice sounds as if it being beamed directly and personally to the individual listener, as if Roberta Flack is just across the room there, conveying her message in a musical combination of science and soul. She is able to catch an audience's attention and hold it to every word as only a few artists can do.

"My gift is to communicate, and I have a great urge to finish what I started back there in Washington with those kids," she said. "I've been working on my doctorate at the University of Massachusetts, studying how to overcome language barriers between students and teachers in inner city schools. One day I'm going to write a guide on how to approach teaching those children. One day I'd like to have a school of my own."

At concerts she warns the young against the use of drugs.

"Progress has to start with the mind. I tell them, and when the mind and reflexes slow down, there's no progress. When drugs wear off, the pain and problems are still there.

"The young, especially the blacks, want to be where I am. They look at me and say, 'She's black, too.'"

"Too many young people think drugs are good, but they have no basis for choosing. Somebody needs to give them alternatives.

"That's what I'm trying to do," said Roberta Flack.

"Music is terribly under-rated as a way to communicate ... People all over the world understand the message, even if there are no words," says Roberta Flack, teacher.

211

Giant African elephant rules Museum Rotunda

An African bush elephant, the largest on record, occupies the Rotunda of the National Museum of Natural History. Shot in Angola in 1955, it weighs eight tons and stands 13 feet two inches at the shoulders. It is believed to be the largest elephant that ever trod the earth.

But even the bush elephant would be dwarfed by dinosaur skeletons, below. The great Diplodocus was 80 feet long. Outside the Museum of History and Technology students, below, compete in races.

The locomotive in the Smithsonian's Railroad Hall is a lovely apparition. Each line in its tremendous length expresses motion. On each side, shining stark against the coal black undercarriage is the silver drive shaft, hinged at the elbow, ready to send three man-tall wheels rolling down the rails. The gold-gleaming bell, red-mouthed as a hound, is eager to swing and ring. The dulled cyclops eye, to send a sword-shaft of light down the track.

The Smithsonian cannily piped in sounds of a locomotive getting under way, the steam hissing, the conductor shouting "Board-d-d-d!," the groaning of couplings, and the slow tramping chuff ...chuff...chuff from the great stack like a giant in boots walking, and, as the mighty drive shafts move faster and the train gains speed the puffing and chuffing picks up tempo and becomes staccato, and the drive shafts are moving so rapidly that they are no more than silver spindles, blurring, and the staccato has become just a scribble of sound, and the headlight is Excaliber swinging back and forth on the curves; and, taking a straight stretch through a valley, against a hillside – remember, it's night – the train is running, gliding, sliding, a black snake banded with lights – and then, what one was waiting for, the huge, hoarse-throated hoot of a whistle, a short one first, then longer, and, finally, a long-drawn wail that throbs through the valley and brings people awake or sends them deeper into dreams, and now the sound of the great train has faded, gone, disappearing into oblivion, and there's nothing but a deep stillness, until, faint but compelling, coming back along the silent track, the long winding wail of the whistle, winding its way across the pastures of a hearer's heart. The middle-aged listen, and, after the sound track is done, shake their heads and walk away.

Alfonso Smith, a guide in the Hall, said old railroad men spend an hour or more at the side of the train.

"They ask me, you know, if they can touch it," he said. "Some of them, the engineers, want to climb in the cab. But we can't let them do that. They might fall out and hurt themselves."

A turn in History and Technology brings you square upon the headquarters tent used by George Washington and his staff. Measing 18 feet by 28 feet, it is of heavy, unbleached, woven linen.

It was the headquarters of the struggling nation as well as the army, because Washington was all that kept it going. The French sent an emissary to size up the situation. He reported that it didn't make any difference how many battles were won or lost, George Washington would never give up. Nothing in American history better illustrates the virtue of hanging on than Washington's staying power. In April 1781, a few months before the Yorktown campaign, he wrote Lafayette: "We are at this hour suspended in the balance... our

213

Foucault pendulum swings 10-foot arc

Extending from the ceiling of the fourth floor almost to the first floor, a 71.5 foot pendulum with a 240-pound hollow brass knob knocks over pegs to demonstrate the earth's rotation. J.B.L. Foucault built the first such pendulum in 1851. The Princeton Stellarator, right, was an early step in nuclear thermal fission. The exhibit, below left, shows use of "influence machine" to treat muscular and nervous disorders by static electricity in 1895. At far right is a covered wagon in Vehicle Hall.

troops are fast approaching to Nakedness ... our hospitals are without medicines and our sick without nutriment ... our public works are at a Stand ... But why need I run into detail, when it may be declared at a word, that we are at the end of our tether, and that now or never our deliverance must come."

It came suddenly. Washington's army slipped way from the New York front, met the French forces under Rochambeau, and dug in with 16,000 troops before Yorktown where British General Cornwallis had 9,000. The move coincided with the arrival in Chesapeake Bay of Admiral de Grasse's French fleet from the West Indies. It cut off Cornwallis from help by sea. Having been forced to spend most of the Revolutionary War avoiding a fight with the British, Washington, at his first opportunity, put it all together in October 1781, at Yorktown.

The siege's climax was the Allie's assault on two outlying redoubts. Lieutenant Colonel Alexander Hamilton led a bayonet charge that cleared Redoubt 10 in 10 minutes and the French stormed Redoubt 9 in half an hour. At his position near the front line, Washington said, "The work is done, and well done."

But, of course, the work wasn't done. When the time came to frame the Constitution in the Philadelphia, they called on him to preside, which he did, mainly in silence for four months, but his presence was steadying. James Monroe wrote Jefferson that he feared that rejection of the Convention's recommendations would mean the country's ruin, but Washington's signature would "secure its passage through the union."

In the same gallery is another striking object, the 71.5 foot Foucault pendulum, extending from the ceiling of the fourth floor almost to the first floor, with a 240-pound hollow brass bob big as a bushel basket and as shiny and pointed as a Christmas tree ornament. The bob swings through a 10-foot arc, never changing its course; but as the earth revolves, and the museum with it, the bob knocks over, one after the other, tiny red pegs arranged in a circle. The shift is so gradual that the bob misses a peg several times by fractions of inches. As it draws nearer the target, a crowd gathers, and when the bob finally hits the peg, there's a vast sigh of relief and even, at times, applause. One man, in his 40s, got down on hands and knees the better to see just how much closer the bob was coming on each successive swing.

An elderly couple watched a while, and she clumped away, muttering, "I'm not going to stand around here. That could make you nervous." But he, a tall fellow with a straight mouth and gimlet eyes, stayed, and when the bob hit the peg, he barked, "Hah!" Many sat on the floor, resting and watching, there was a sense of Christmas morning with a new toy about the scene. One kneeling youth had a child in a backpack and as the great golden orb swung back and forth, the infant's eyes suddenly focused. For how many years, one wondered, will that shining, swinging image haunt his mind and elude his memory. The first such pendulum was built by the French physicist J.B.L. Foucault in 1851, as a sort of giant show-and-tell to demonstrate that the earth turns on its axis.

But a man can get enough of even History and Technology. He sat on the bench, shoulders bowed, his big, rubbery mouth disconsolate, his straw hat shoved back on his bald head. Around him, in various stage of collapse, were three children. His wife, however, sat bolt upright, grim-mouthed.

"Don't forget," he said, wheedling, "we did some walking this morning. We didn't only come here. If you can only say you've been here when you get home – You can say, 'Yeah, I was there!'"

She didn't open her mouth, didn't budge.

They could, he pleaded, stop and eat a hamburger on the way to the motel. A boy, about 10, came from the gallery below, returning like the dove to the Ark.

"Anything special?" asked his mother.

There would be, one felt, whatever the report.

In the Rotunda of the National Museum of Natural History is a huge African bush elephant, the largest on record, perhaps the largest ever to tread the earth, slain in 1955 in Angola, Africa by J.J. Fenykovi. The Smithsonian worked two years to restore it.

The elephant dominates the center of the great round room, his trunk curled high for a trumpet call, the ivory tusks long as a man, his triangular ears spread broad as sails, his eyes red with hate, caught in just the moment of his swinging stride across the plain.

The customary image of an elephant is a placid beggar sweeping the ground with languid trunk for peanuts. The ruler of the Rotunda is wild. His trunk is gnarled as an oak, crusted as a barnacled timber, and his tail ends in a great brush. Nothing sags in his bulk. He is all streamlined might. Like a massive mountain, he offers a new aspect at every turn. Weighing 12 tons – the horned rhino at the zoo weighs, at most, only four tons – standing 13 feet two inches at the shoulders, he approaches the dimensions of the legendary mammoth.

A father stood reading to his son, about 4, the dimensions of the stupendous beast, and, when he finished, the boy had a question.

"If it was so big," he asked, "why did they kill it?"

Every Fourth of July weekend the Smithsonian and the National Park Service are hosts to the Annual Festival of American Folklife. A family reunion for the nation, it lines both sides of the Reflecting Pool before the Lincoln Memorial.

Father Abraham, looking down, sees his children on the move: streaming back and forth between the two sides of the Mall, one vast, pulsating organism; heads, seal-dark, swimming across the Reflecting Pool; the raft, loaded, being pulled back and forth, a crudely articulated sea serpent; a man, about 40, lying flat on his back on the Memorial's cool stone, a camera resting precisely in the center of his stomach, saying to his wife, who isn't paying attention: "It feels so good to lay down."

And smells them: the sweat, hot dogs and hamburgers broiling, spicy fragrances of Old World dishes, exhausts from grinding buses, and vinegar being daubed by a child's mother on its insect bites.

And hears them: a mother calling, "Let's go, hon!", a fiddle wailing, footfalls, never ending, up and down his steps, sandals slapping, the thump of bare heels, the soft sound of sneakers, the click-clack of high heels, the yammering of auctioneers, the whine of a harmonica, and another mother calling: "Brad, you can't slide down that slide, anymore!"

His memorial is a hospitable lap for people.

Among people at the Festival weaving, quilting, chopping wood, and otherwise conducting themselves industriously, one man, 83-year-old Ray Lum of Vicksburg, was just talking. A crowd was always listening, as if weaned on TV, they had never heard anybody talk.

In string tie and straw hat, red-faced Lum started talking in the morning, as soon as the Festival stirred to life, and talked the sun right down the sky, drawing from his 75 years as a trader of horses, mules and anything else, because, as he said in a magnificent quadruple negative, "a real trader don't never find nothing he can't use." From his experience as an auctioneer, he began expatiating on horses and mules: "A horse is stronger, but a mule's a better worker because he never balks. You get a horse scared, and he'll jump in water or go over a cliff, but you run a mule up to a cliff, and you may go over, but that mule ain't; he'll stop. When there's any danger, any caving, you can't get a mule up close to it. But a horse – you can pull a horse out of a burning barn, and he'll break loose from you and run back in the barn to burn – oh, my God, it's awful.

"I remember at Vicksburg there were some mules owned by the city when the municipal barn caught fire at 1 o'clock in the morning. They got them all out, but one mule had caught fire, a big white mule worked by an old darky, who thought a lot of her. So the mule started burning. The old darky was home in bed a mile away, and that mule, because he had looked after her at the city barn, went all the way down to his house, just burning up. That's the most pitiful thing I ever witnessed with a mule. She loved that old darky, and he loved her. And he never did work for the city anymore."

In the late afternoon a crowd began collecting at the Indian encampment to watch the foot-

Thousands bask in opera, sun at Wolf Trap

Music lovers listen to the Metropolitan Opera open the summer season for Wolf Trap Farm, the first national park for the performing arts. Catherine Shouse gave the 100 acres and funded the building of Filene Center, which is named for her parents.

218

*Filene Center, the heart
of Wolf Trap Farm, is
located in Fairfax County,
near Dulles Airport,
17 miles from Washington.
The Center seats 3,500
under cover and 3,000 on
the sloping lawn. The
stage house is 10 stories
high; the stage is 100
feet wide, 64 feet deep,
spacious enough for
the most spectacular pro-
ductions during the
12-week summer season. It
opened July, 1971 and
has been busy ever since.*

Filene Center has full house plus outdoors

Ford, party open season at Wolf Trap

Celebrating the opening of Wolf Trap Farm's summer season, guests at a reception, far left, roam the green lawns. In a pavilion Gerald Ford, then Vice President, prepares to open champagne. Looking on, upper left, are Mrs. Shouse, Governor Mills Godwin of Virginia, and Mrs. Henry Jackson. Melvin Laird, chairman of Wolf Trap Farm Foundation, appears, lower left, to join Ford's moment of triumph at the opening.

Indians dance at the Annual Folk Festival

Indian boys from New Mexico ran from the Lincoln Memorial to the Capitol and back and seemed scarcely winded.

Young and old redmen dance and sing at an evening pow wow on the Mall at the Annual Festival of American Folklife sponsored by the Smithsonian Institution. The Festival, an annual birthday party for the nation, usually starts the Fourth of July weekend, but a summer-long celebration was in store for the Bicentennial year of 1976. The Indians are from the Native American area. Other countries are in Old Ways in the New World.

stamping dances and seize some vestige, bright as beadwork, of their life style.

A clear, little noticed, demonstration of it was in the long distance running of five youths from Laguna Acoma Junior and Senior High Schools in New Mexico.

They set out running from the Lincoln Memorial to the Capitol and back, their black hair tossing, glossy as rooster tails, and when they topped the rise toward the Washington Monument, the dark, lithe, running figures silhouetted against the sky, looked as Indian as the finest of their forefathers.

In 26 minutes they returned, faces slick with sweat but breathing about as hard as a person who's made a dash for a bus.

They run, they said, early in the morning, then in the afternoon, and then after hours. (Their names: Meldon Sanchez, Bruce Romero, Joe Gordon, Emmett Hunt, and Steve Cachupin.)

And what did they think about as they ran?

"We don't look around at trees," said one, smiling.

Well, why run?

There was a pause, and one said, "We're here."

Where?

"D.C.," he said.

Busiest feature at the Folklife Festival was a Family Folklore tent directed by a graduate student from the University of Pennsylvania, Steven Zeitlin.

The Smithsonian's senior folklorist, Bob Byington, encouraged public participation in the Festival, and Zeitlin suggested that families be invited to tape their own recollections.

There were small items, names of cars – Nellie was a popular name and 1947, right after the war, was a big year for buying the family car – and historical events. They talked it all into recorders.

"Of all the events, the one that had the greatest impact was the Civil War," said Zeitlin, "It's interesting that more than 100 years later, the profound effect is still manifest.

"The Depression also comes up again and again, but often in a curiously negative way. The children know their parents had been scarred very badly, but it's something they never talked about."

He remembered a woman in her 60s who was on the way to take her 85-year-old father fishing.

"At their age," he said, "they were still making up fresh folklore about their lives.

"She did tell me one habit from the past that I thought expressed her zest for life. Ever since she was a child on the first day of spring she had bathed before sun up in the fresh water of a lake or a stream."

The reminiscencies will find there way eventually into a Smithsonian publication.

Outside the folklore tent, standing on a sawdust walk, two men discussed the difficulties of driving in Washington, for themselves, not the Smithsonian.

"I can get in it all right," said the first, "but I can't ever get out."

"What you got to do," advised the other, "is when you have a choice, always take the road leading *away* from where you want to go."

The National Gallery of Art, extending 780 feet in length, is the largest marble structure in the world; and, a cab driver noted, the marble turns rose in the rain. The bronze doors roll back, thunderously, like a cliff parting for the Pied Piper, and visitors, streaming inside, are engulfed by the Rotunda as if they had entered a redwood forest. Here one can wander down the corridors of civilization.

For children there is "Daniel in the Lions' Den" by Peter Paul Rubens, a gift through the Ailsa Mellon Bruce Fund, spreading across an entire wall. There are, if one counts carefully, 11 lions. It takes a good deal of arranging to get 11 lions in one space without there seeming to be a pyramid of them, like Clyde Beatty's old act. But Rubens managed it, he tamed 'em, and the lions and their flowing manes and rippling muscles tumble over the rocks of the den like tawny waters spilling down a rapids. You can almost smell the musky odor of the lions and feel the fetid air of the den in which Daniel sits, his hands folded in prayer, and looks up at the den's mouth through which the cool light of the morning is pouring, a libation bathing his figure.

For youths there is a painting by Jean-Honore Fragonard of a young girl reading, dressed in lemony satin, auburn hair pulled back in a knot from her innocent features, rosy-cheeked, pampered, protected, altogether lovely, reading, from the looks of it, Voltaire's *Candide* – which probably will turn her against her parents, class, and society.

For those growing older there is a self-portrait of Rembrandt at 53 in the Andrew W. Mellon Collection. The great painter's eyes are sad and deeply knowledgeable, steady, pained, dark, looking through himself without vanity – and through and through the viewer.

For everybody there is the so-called Vaughan portrait of the Father of Our Country by Gilbert Stuart. Portraits of Washington hang all over the city, including three in the Capitol. One worth tracking down is the so-called Thomas Chestnut portrait, done by Gilbert Stuart, in the Senate Conference Room. Stuart painted some 40 Washingtons.

Familiar to most Americans is the Athenaeum portrait, left unfinished, so that, hanging on schoolroom walls, mists seem to be rising about him, or myths, out of Parson Weems.

Stuart, writing of one sitting, said an apathy seemed to seize Washington, "and a vacuity spread over his countenance most appalling to

Annual Folklife Festival spreads along the Mall

Exhibits line both sides of the Reflecting Pool, and a raft ferries visitors to and fro. Sam Chapman of Hollandale, Mississippi plays a broom handle, lower left, and auctioneer Ray Lum holds a crowd spellbound with endless stories.

paint." Stuart tried in vain, to "awaken the heroic spirit" in him by talking of battles. "Forget for a moment or two, you are President of the United States," suggested Stuart. Washington's step-son said that Washington retorted: "I'll not forget that I am President; don't you forget you're a painter."

Into a press conference at the Smithsonian Institution came the three astronauts – Neil Armstrong, Edwin Aldrin Jr., and Michael Collins – on July 20, 1974, the fifth anniversary of their flight to the moon. Their appearance recalled how those on earth felt a certain weightlessness, too, on July 20, 1969, when Eagle, the lunar vehicle, sat on the moon.

It looked like something put together with an Erector Set and Tinker Toys, or an assemblage of loose boards, rusty softdrink signs, and old stove pipe hammered, wind-blown, into a treetop. Its hatch opened, and a foot appeared, felt cautiously, withdrew, and then stepped on the first rung of the ladder. The lower half of astronaut Armstrong backed into view, the way children, taught by their mothers on earth, turn to come downstairs backwards, using all fours. Thus, Armstrong came down the ladder and stepped onto the moon. His first words were not a simple whew, we made it, or a shout of joy; but, like a boy reciting his one, oft-rehearsed line in a school play, he said: "One small step for a man, one giant leap for mankind."

Five years later the three astronauts sat on the Smithsonian's stage. Aldrin remembered that on the moon's surface he had reflected how much farther away from home they were than they had ever been, and yet how close they were to those watching on earth.

On the flight to the moon, said Armstrong, he had "a continual suspicion that the next item on the check list would be the one that would conk out. It was always a great pleasure to find something else that worked."

From the start of the space venture, the spectators in front of TV sets had been surprised when things worked, especially in the early blastoffs when they tensed, not knowing if the rocket would go up or over. When, white clouds billowing at the base of the craft, the liftoff came, so slowly that the rocket seemed to hover a moment, straining, and then, finally soared free, people in homes and offices cheered and wiped their eyes.

Patriotism was keenest in the United States just after the Russians orbited Sputnik in 1957. Americans tend to take success for granted, and by 1969 the rejoicing at the moon walk was largely for the sake of the human race, not the United States.

At the Smithsonian, Collins noted that American astronauts and Soviet cosmonauts got along well together. A joint space program might bridge

It is possible on the Mall to pet a dinosaur, at least a reconstructed one stationed before the National Museum of Natural History. Inside, it is possible to touch a real dinosaur bone; but one tired son, right, prefers his father's shoulder.

Children romp on triceratops along the Mall

Spacemen stand by moon module "Columbia"

On the fifth anniversary of their flight to the moon, astronauts Edwin Aldrin, Michael Collins, and Neil Armstrong stand in the Smithsonian's Air and Space Museum before the Apollo 11 command module Columbia. On July 20, 1969, Aldrin and Armstrong walked on the moon. Five years later they said they were surprised and pleased that all went well. Above the Columbia is the Kitty Hawk Flyer. In it the Wright brothers became the first to fly a heavier-than-air plane. Early rockets rise, right, with the spires of the Arts and Industries Museum.

228

chasms, he suggested, because "on a technical basis, it's very much easier to agree whether something is so or not." Aldrin thought the landing's significance was "that we accepted the challenge ... an extension of the wanderlust we've had through our history."

While the astronauts were on the lunar surface, Americans went out in the night, and looked up at the pale gold, pocked sphere, and felt, seeing it remote and serene, more sharply than at any time they had watched the proceedings on television, the wonder that men were walking ant-like across the moon's face. Taking the dare offered by the young President, gearing up, the country had done it.

And having done that, why not, many questioned, attend things that need doing on earth? Well, it's an open society, increasingly, for marshaling support. And the resource for testing and implementing an idea is ready in the machinery of checks and balances the framers put together and their followers continue to adjust. The Declaration and the Constitution are as vibrant as the day they were born.

Thomas Jefferson, as always, put it best. The citizens of the City of Washington invited him to join them in observing the 50th anniversary of the Declaration of Independence. Ten days before he died, in the last letter he wrote, Jefferson answered.

Their kind invitation was most flattering, he said, and it added to his sufferings to be deprived by sickness "of a personal participation in the rejoicings of that day..." And then, spirit flaring, he added:

"May it be to the world what I believe it will be (to some parts sooner, or to others later, but finally to all) the signal of arousing men to burst the chains under which monkish ignorance and superstition had persuaded them to bind themselves, and to assume the blessings and security of self-government. That form which we have substituted restores the free right to the unbounded exercise of reason and freedom of opinion.

"All eyes are opened, or opening, to the rights of man. The general spread of the light of science has already laid open to every view the palpable truth that the mass of mankind has not been born with saddles on their backs, nor a favored few booted and spurred, ready to ride them legitimately by the grace of God. These are grounds of hope for others. For ourselves, let the annual return of this day forever refresh our recollection of these rights, and an undiminished devotion to them."

On the 200th anniversary the bright hope lies with the Capitol — and, close by, the Supreme Court and the White House — sitting widespread under the wide skies above the open city of Washington.

229

The Capitol rules the Mall: left, domed National Gallery of Art; lower right, Smithsonian Castle, circular Hirsh

horn, three-part Air and Space Museum. Behind Capitol, left, is Supreme Court; right, Library of Congress.

Other books by BURDA

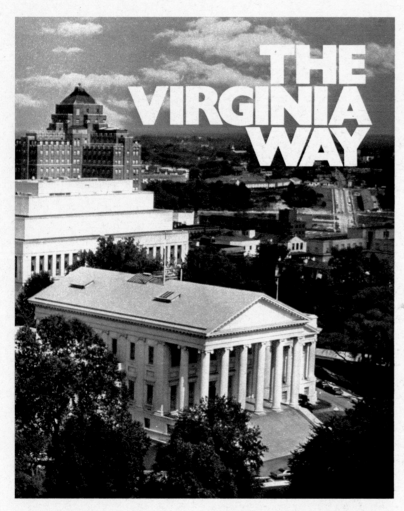

THE VIRGINIA WAY

Thomas Jefferson defined "The Virginia Way." Guy Friddell and Wolfgang Roth illustrate its survival. 232 pages, 114 color photographs, 85 black & white photographs.

FLORIDA A PLACE IN THE SUN

The sun presides, in varying degrees of attention, over all Florida. Al Burt and Heinz Erhardt explore that unique peninsula in words and pictures.